CHEVROLET

A HISTORY FROM 1911

AN AUTOMOBILE QUARTERLY MARQUE HISTORY BOOK

Those most instrumental in creating the Chevrolet gathered together in Detroit for the inauguration of the Classic Six. Third from left, in white coat, is Louis Chevrolet. B

...rant, in top hat, stands at left of windshield; his son Cliff is at the wheel.

A HISTORY FROM 1911

BY BEVERLY RAE KIMES
AND
ROBERT C. ACKERSON

PRODUCED BY THE STAFF OF
AUTOMOBILE QUARTERLY MAGAZINE

AUTOMOBILE QUARTERLY PUBLICATIONS

EDITORIAL & PRODUCTION STAFF

Editor: Lowell C. Paddock
Associate Editors: John F. Katz, Julie M. Fenster
Art Director: Michael Pardo
Associate Art Director: David W. Bird II
Production Editor: Deborah Morrison
Editorial Assistant: Patricia H. Lincoln
Maketing Director: Stephen E. Pearson

Editor for this Book: Lowell C. Paddock
Founding Publisher: L. Scott Bailey

SECOND EDITION

Chapters One through Five of this book first appeared as a series of articles in AUTOMOBILE *Quarterly* magazine in the following editions and are copyrighted by Automobile Quarterly Publications: Volume XVIII, Number 3; Volume XVIII, Number 4; Volume XIX, Number 1; Volume XIX, Number 2; and Volume XIX, Number 4.

Typesetting by Kutztown Publishing Company, Kutztown, Pennsylvania
Color Separations by Lincoln Graphics, Inc., Cherry Hill, New Jersey
Printing and Binding by South China Printing Co., Ltd., Hong Kong

ISBN 0-915038-62-5: Automobile Quarterly, Inc.

Library of Congress Catalog Number: 86-062128

CONTENTS

PREFACE   6

PREFACE

The Eighties have been a decade of important automotive anniversaries. General Motors commemorated seventy-five years of delivering automobiles to the world in 1982. Four years later, Mercedes-Benz basked in the glory surrounding the centennial of the automobile's very creation. And now it is Chevrolet's turn to celebrate seventy-five years of putting America on wheels, and it's an anniversary that's close to the American heart.

"Baseball, hot dogs, apple pie and Chevrolet" was a jingle heard frequently by television and radio audiences throughout the country during 1975 and 1976. Chevrolet's campaign served to remind the car-conscious consumer that Chevrolet was really very close to the pulse of America's heart. Of course, as with any really successful advertisement, it was based on the truth.

While the gentlemen from Dearborn might object that their vehicles, by virtue of their visionary creator, are more American yet, Chevrolet can always point to its sales figures, which show that for the past seventy-five years it has outsold every other single car maker in the world. But Chevrolet's strength lies in breadth as well as depth. Its product lines in the Sixties and Seventies, for example, encompassed an astonishing variety of automobiles, far more than any of its competitors, within GM or without. In 1966, Chevrolet went into battle girded with the evergreen Impala on one flank and the humble Nova on the other. In between lay the Corvette, Corvair and Chevelle. A decade later, there would be an even broader range, including the Camaro, Monte Carlo, Monza and Vega. Only the Corvair had been dropped from the ranks.

But being on top has had its disquieting moments. With such quantities being turned out each day, a minor mistake can create a gargantuan headache. Indeed, throughout the postwar era, Chevrolet's most challenging problem has been keeping up with its own success. Though no ill intent was planned, the growing intrusion of cost concerns into design and engineering created fragile compromises that risked falling apart soon after leaving the showroom. While the '55 Chevrolet

produced a nation of eager fans, owners of Vegas with self-destructing engines and dissolving sheet metal found their confidence in Chevrolet's ability to deliver a high quality product severely shaken. But just as Chevrolet recovered from the copper cooling debacle, so too did it recover from these more modern problems. The Vega soon gave way to the Cavalier, whose hard-earned reputation has made it an American best-seller.

Decades earlier, *Fortune* had noted that Chevorlet's very success derived from its having "fewer enemies than any car made . . . [it is] the greatest common denominator of what the American public thinks a good car ought to be." While that statement may have been an oversimplification, it underscored Chevrolet's ability to create new products, manufacture them in staggering quantities, get the American public to snap them up, and do it all again the following year, often in even greater quantities. Just getting one part of that recipe performed properly was challenge enough. That Chevrolet could do it all in greater numbers than Ford—or anyone else for that matter—year after year wasn't just miraculous, it was and remains incredible.

While many of Chevrolet's problems have been generated by the twin hurdles of high volume production and government regulation, a third was created by the emergence of Japan as a major world automaker. The growing popularity of reliable, efficient and inexpensive Japanese automobiles clashed directly with Chevrolet's mission, that of being the largest provider of transportation for the low-priced segment of the American market. And as Detroit discovered in the dark days of the late Seventies, it was going to take a lot more than searchlights, headlines and giveaways to sell cars. Consumers had become more demanding, making the marketplace more competitive. What had once been just three big friendly kids on the block became a horde converging on the U.S. from around the globe, all jostling for the price-conscious consumer's attention. After some hoping that the problem might go away, Chevrolet finally concluded that joining them would be a lot more productive than trying to beat them. And so now Chevrolet brings 150,000 Japanese cars to these shores, in addition to building 200,000 hybrid automobiles here.

With that mission successfully accomplished, Chevrolet faces a new challenge: to successfully launch the domestically produced Corsica and Beretta in a fiercely competitive automobile market. Aware of the problems involved, Chevrolet is going to great lengths to insure that these two cars find and keep a willing market. As if the construction of over 544 pilot cars was not enough, the actual introduction of the car will be a two-step process, beginning with daily rental car companies and then actual dealer introduction.

Just how well these two new cars will fare is a story that remains to be told, but seventy-five years of transportation experience is solid ground upon which to build. Recent experience bodes well for the future, as the Cavalier and Celebrity have become two of the best-selling cars in America. The Camaro seems to find an ever-larger audience each year as well, while the Corvette continues to make a name for itself in the world of high performance.

Helping to maintain this tide of success in a changed world is the mandate of a staff of thousands, each of whom must take considerable pride in Chevrolet's progress. The strong glue of commitment and ability that continues to hold the Chevrolet reputation together has been in ample supply since the company's earliest days, and has extended down from the general manager to the green salesman closing his first deal. Any roster of great automotive pioneers would surely include a sampling of Chevrolet's engineering and marketing leaders: Billy Durant, Alfred Sloan, Jr., Charles Kettering, William S. Knudsen, Ed Cole and Zora Arkus-Duntov, just to name a few.

Since its creation in 1962, Automobile Quarterly has published dozens of articles and several books on the legacy of Chevrolet. *Corvette: America's Star-Spangled Sports Car* by Karl Ludvigsen was the first detailed history of the Corvette. It was followed by a volume on the best articles from *Corvette News,* Restoration guides for 1953-1962 and 1963-1967 Corvettes, *A Piece of the Action, Corvette: An American Legend* and *The Legend Lives On,* all full-color tributes to the glory of the Corvette and *Corvette! Thirty Years of Great Advertising.* Summing up the history of GM overall was *General Motors: The First Seventy-Five Years*, a complete retrospective on the world's mightiest industrial powerhouse.

The first half of this book, written by Beverly Rae Kimes, appeared originally as a series of articles in *Automobile Quarterly* magazine. The response was such that a book on the entire history of Chevrolet was planned. To write the second half we turned to Chevrolet historian Robert C. Ackerson, who assembled the complicated history of Chevrolet from 1955 on.

None of this would have been possible without the assistance of virtually hundreds of individuals within the Chevrolet Motor Division. Although space does not allow us to thank everyone individually, the authors and editors are indebted to: Ralph Kramer, Ed Lechtzin, Duane Poole, Suzanne Kane, Nancy Libby, Kay Ward, Arlene Reindel and Joe Tori of the Chevrolet Public Relations Department; Robert Lund, Robert Stempel, Tom McDaniel, Bob de Kruyff, the late Vince Piggins, Clare MacKichan, Robert Eaton, Doug Roe, Paul Prior and Walter McKenzie, all present or former Chevrolet employees; Dave Holls, Chuck Jordon, Roger Hughet and Jerry Palmer of General Motors; and the late Jim Bradley of the National Automotive History Collection.

Finally, I would like to thank all the Chevrolet owners and Chevrolet clubs who volunteered their automobiles for photography. The time, money and love they expend on their cars is the best testament to Chevrolet's greatness.

Lowell C. Paddock
Princeton, New Jersey 7

CHAPTER ONE

LAUNCHING THE CHEVROLET

The Early Years of the Marque

Once, when asked whether he ever worried, he replied that he didn't, because during the day he was too busy and at night he was too tired.

In truth, when night fell, he was generally still too busy. Frederick L. Smith would remember that when he negotiated the purchase of the Olds Motor Works for the new company he was forming, that it was "on the sleepy side of midnight, but all hours were business hours to Bill." The two of them toured the factory at 3:00 a.m.

Some months later when he decided to buy Cadillac, and put the matter before its board of directors, one of the members was the same Fred Smith. "I'd like to go along with you, Bill," Fred Smith said, "but you know you still owe my father $1,800,000 from the last deal you made."

"Great Scott, I'd forgotten all about it," Billy Durant said.

And nobody doubted that he had. The fact of nearly two million dollars was as unlikely of recall as the reality that most business days ended at 5:00 p.m. He didn't worry about money either.

Had he wished to acknowledge it, there was really a lot he had to worry about now. He had lost his business. The bankers had arrived and taken General Motors away from him. The company was a "paying proposition," they decided, "its only trouble having been over-enthusiasm on the part of its managers."

It was just before Thanksgiving in the year 1910.

"He now is in the toils of Wall Street, so to speak, and must do its bidding. . .," *Motor World* wrote of Billy Durant. "The feeling is . . . that an element of real peril has been circumvented and chastened." Circumvented, maybe. Chastened? Never.

With all the sanguinity he could muster, he accepted a vice-presidency and took the seat on the GM board of directors that the bankers had offered him. They thought he couldn't cause much trouble there, and they set about immediately trying to undo a lot of what Billy had done, sorting out the "scrap heap," as one of them put it. It was a characterization he always resented—and one only partially true. "I try never to make the same mistake twice" was all Billy said. He said it positively, not apologetically.

Billy Durant never could resist a bargain. In bringing together the flurry of companies wearing the GM banner, he had occasionally made a "peach of a deal" that turned out to be a lemon. He recognized belatedly, for example, the judgmental error he had made in purchasing John Heany's company for $7 million in GM stock and $112,759 in cash—more than the combined expenditure required for the purchase of Olds and the bringing into the GM fold of the Buick company he had made such a smashing success of in Flint. Heany had improved the electric light bulb—or so Heany said, and sought to patent some of his ideas. Unfortunately, Heany also fudged a little on his patent application to give a false priority of date. The General Electric company noticed, and so did the Patent Office. The former sued, the latter turned the facts over to federal attorneys. In the meantime, Billy had bought the Heany company.

The patents were subsequently declared worthless, the estimated loss to GM was figured around that time to range up to $12 million—with the compounding

William C. Durant

of dividends awarded original stockholders through the years, the figure would be put at over $370 million in the late Twenties—and Billy Durant decided it's not always wise to do business with a man who's been under indictment. An easy mistake not to make twice.*

Besides, he really knew more about cars than about light bulbs anyway. True, he had bought the Cartercar company but, as he had lamented to a friend, "How was anyone to know the Cartercar wasn't the thing? It had friction drive and no other car had it. How could I tell what these engineers would say next?" But about the future of the automobile itself, he had no question.

And on that subject he thought the bankers who had taken GM away from him were now making mistakes. They had seen fit to discontinue the Model 10— the most successful Buick he had ever introduced—and seemed to be moving in the direction of more powerful and more expensive automobiles. That was entirely wrong. There were other companies in General Motors to build such cars. Indeed when he bought Olds and found it "was losing money and needed a lower-priced car quickly," had he not taken a Model 10 Buick body from Flint to Lansing, ordered it sawed in half lengthwise and crosswise, put it on an Olds chassis and "so by stretching the Buick body and finishing it in different paint we had a new small Oldsmobile that sold for $1200."

Bankers didn't understand marketing. He was sure of that. Nor did they comprehend the coming prominence of the automobile in America. A few years earlier, when he had approached Wall Street for additional funding to expand his Buick and Cadillac plants, he was asked what the large vacant space on the blueprints was for.

"To park cars," Billy had replied.

"What cars?"

"The cars of the workmen."

The banker was aghast. "Do you mean to tell me, Mr. Durant, that ordinary factory employees will drive automobiles?"

No, bankers didn't know automobiles. They wouldn't be convinced if he told them what a success he had made of his Durant-Dort company before the turn of the century by building low-priced buggies instead of high-priced carriages. They wouldn't be convinced either if he told them what Henry Ford was trying to do with the Model T. Henry Ford hated bankers. And he had said so in print. Billy Durant didn't hate them. But he didn't respect them. And he saw no way he could work with them congenially.

"With no idea of being disloyal, it seemed to me that it would be better to let the new group handle the business to suit themselves," he concluded, "and if I ever expected to regain control of General Motors, which I certainly intended to

*There is another view of this episode which holds that buying the Heany company was not a mistake at all, that Durant was aware of the problems but made the purchase anyway as part of a stock-watering plan. This seems most unlikely, in this writer's view, given Durant's other moves during this period. Probably his enthusiasm simply ran away with his ego. Putting together General Motors had made him very cocky.

1912 Chevrolet Six Type C Classic / Owner: M.G. "Pinky" Randall, on display loan to the Alfred P. Sloan, Jr. Museum, Flint

1912 Little Four / Owner: M.G. "Pinky" Randall, on display loan to the Alfred P. Sloan, Jr. Museum, Flint

1914 Type H-2 Royal Mail Roadster / Owner: M.G. "Pinky" Randall

1914 Type H-4 Baby Grand Touring / Owner: Wayne McKinley

1914 Type H-4 Baby Grand Touring / Owner: M.G. "Pinky" Randall

do, I should have a company of my own, run in my own way. In other words, another one-man institution, but taking a leaf out of Henry Ford's book—No bankers."

In 1911 there were 270 automobile manufacturers in the United States. By 1915 the number was halved, as Darwin S. Hatch noted in *Motor Age* that year. In retrospect, that writer's first name seems peculiarly appropriate. The survival of the fittest in the automobile industry would mean the halving of manufacturers in the field again and again as the years progressed. From the hundreds of pre-World War I, there would be the handful of post-World War II. And the ranks would continue to be diminished.

The "one-man institution" Billy Durant began in 1911 was called Chevrolet.

Of all the personalities who contributed to the foundations of the American automobile industry, none was a more compelling and complex man than William Crapo Durant. He was perhaps too short in stature to be called dashing, and he was too well born to be a Horatio Alger. But, still, there was always a sense of the romantic about him, and a rags-to-riches—and back and forth again—aura followed him for the whole of his career. He was an adventurer, in every meaning of the word. He was emotional, with boundless enthusiasm and deep sensitivity. He could hide neither. He cried shamelessly once while watching Raymond Massey portray Lincoln on the New York stage. He bubbled over always when he talked of new ventures. "He could charm a bird right down out of a tree," Walter Chrysler once said of Billy Durant.

He'd been doing it for a long time already. He was the grandson of Henry Howland Crapo, a Michigan lumber magnate and two-term governor of that state. His father was William Clark Durant, who exercised little moderation in either consumption of liquor or speculation in stock and who one day, as Durant biographers of that era put it, "went fishing"—doubtless in the figurative not the literal sense—and never came back. Young Billy would not inherit one of his father's traits; he seldom drank, and never to excess. Although at one point he did hire detectives to find his father, it was his mother to whom he was utterly devoted—psycho-historians might infer it was oedipal—for the rest of her long life, and it was from Rebecca Crapo Durant that he drew strong character traits of determination, loyalty, honesty.

And he was blessed—parentage seemed to have played no part—with what can only be described as the colossal ability to sell anything. And almost anyone. He peddled patent medicines early in his career, cigars a little later. He sold insurance and real estate. He sold J. Dallas Dort on joining him in the carriage business, and a lot of people in Flint into investing in an automobile company that had not yet built more than about three dozen Buicks. He sold the Smiths on the handing over of Olds, and the Lelands on the contribution of Cadillac, to the new idea he called General Motors. Among many others.

The only people he couldn't sell, he seemed, were the bankers. And when they stopped him, he had another idea to sell and someone else to sell it to. He went to the garage at 3939 Grand River Avenue in Detroit and asked to see Louis.

Louis Chevrolet and Bob Burman had been the stalwarts of the Buick racing team, the *modus operandi* by which Billy Durant had so effectively promoted the Buick name during the marque's early production years in Flint. The Buick competition record had been the envy of the industry. "Wild" Bob was still racing but Louis was by now given to sporadic announcements of his impending retirement from the sport—and Billy was aware of Chevrolet's interest in 13 becoming an automobile designer. To Durant, he seemed perfect for the job. He had tinkered with and tuned various of the Buick race cars, though he had never before designed a motorcar; probably the only complete product of his invention thus far had been the wine pump he had run up as boy in France. (Swiss-born, the son of a clockmaker, Louis had moved with his family to the grape-growing region of Burgundy when he was five, and emigrated to America seventeen years later.)

It seems likely that what Durant liked most about Chevrolet was his name, both for the prominence it enjoyed in motor sport and for the simple fact that he liked the sound of it. Years earlier he had liked the euphony of David Dunbar Buick's name too, though he worried that people might pronounce it boo-ick. He had already decided to solve any such problem in this new venture by seeing to it that Louis' last name was spelled phonetically as well as actually on billboards until such time as it became engrained in the public consciousness.

But first he had to have a car, and he put Chevrolet to work. Chevrolet in turn enlisted the support of Frenchman Etienne Planche whom he had met while both were working in William Walter's Brooklyn motor shops during their early emigré years in America. This seemed logical too. Not only had Planche already designed a car (the Roebling-Planche, antecedent to the Mercer), but Durant's specifications were for a vehicle along "French light car" lines and both men knew what that meant.

No one at this point knew what Durant was doing. Several months later, on May 30th, 1911, however, a Detroit newspaper story linked the two men together in the impending establishment of a factory in Detroit to build a "Durant-Chevrolet car . . . of high grade"—and mentioned that Louis that day would be driving a Buick in the inaugural Indianapolis 500. He did, but he retired early on with a broken crankshaft—and he retired immediately after to his garage and the drawing board.

Interestingly, six weeks later, on July 20th, the New York-based publication *Motor World* thought it had a real scoop. Headlining the news "Durant Assisting New Venture" on page one, the story mentioned "the formation of what will be styled the Chevrolet Motor Car Company" for the manufacture of "a high-powered speed car designed by Louis Chevrolet" and quoted the company's "organizer" William H. Little to the effect that "Durant will be one of its officers, or at any rate, he can be one, if he so desires." Perhaps *Motor World* editors hadn't noticed the Detroit newspaper Memorial Day article indicating the much closer Durant-Chevrolet alliance. Or perhaps since it had been *Motor World* which had referred to Billy as the "element of real peril" in the General Motors situation, the Durant forces had not been overly anxious to provide accurate information.

But in the months to follow until the end of 1911, too much would be happening to be kept under cover—and Billy was ready to go public with his plans now in any case. It was apparent almost immediately that the new Durant venture was virtually a Buick alumni reunion.

First to be incorporated, on July 31st, 1911, was the Mason Motor Company in Flint, named for Arthur C. Mason, a Buick engineer from the early days. Billy bought the Flint Wagon Works factory from an aging and anxious-to-retire James H. Whiting, who had been one of the early Buick financial angels—and told Mason he would be building engines there for Durant's new motorcars.

The plural is intentional. For next to be incorporated, on October 30th, 1911,

1915 Type H-3 Amesbury Special / Owner: Mrs. Jack Munitz

was the Little Motor Car Company which would share space with Mason in the old wagon works and produce a small and inexpensive car to be named for Durant's former general manager at Buick, the aforementioned William H. Little.

Finally, on November 8th, 1911, the Chevrolet Motor Car Company was incorporated, again with former Buick people named as officers and Curtis R. Hatheway, who had filed the GM incorporation papers in 1908, as secretary. Durant secured the plant of the Corcoran Lamp Company on West Grand for that venture's immediate premises, and bought about forty acres of land to the north for its permanent location and a new five-story factory. A billboard on the site announced the imminent arrival there of the Chevrolet, and *The Horseless Age* announced two weeks later that the Lansing men imported to clear the land had upon arrival "struck for 2½ cents more per hour. Thereupon the contractor sent them flying and secured Detroit laborers to do the work." It was never completed, Durant ultimately deciding to concentrate Michigan Chevrolet manufacture in Flint. This was rather a shame, in a way. The site was directly across the street from the Ford Motor Company.*

Meanwhile, as the Lansing woodchoppers were striking in Detroit, Billy Durant was in Flint attending a gala banquet in his honor at which male guests were offered after-dinner Flint-made cigars with their bands reading "El Capitan de Industria" from cigar boxes with Billy Durant's picture on the top and a gilded decorative design worthy of the best from Havana. No one had seen anything of any new car yet. But no one worried. The Flint feast had been entitled "The Wizard's Banquet."

Six weeks later the Wizard sent Bill Little to Detroit to try to hurry up Louis Chevrolet who was still at the drawing board, and entrusted the coming production of the Little in Flint to Alexander Brownell Cullen Hardy, who preferred being called A.B.C. or Alex and who had been an officer in the Durant-Dort Carriage Company before the turn of the century and with Billy later in General Motors. Hardy arrived at his new job to find Arthur Mason and his engine operation in the best part of the factory, the Little consigned to an area littered with everything from wooden wagons to whip sockets. These and other paraphernalia of the horse-drawn age, he was informed, should be sold off to bring in some extra money.

The Little operation was classically shoestring. Its announced capitalization of $1.2 million was impressive enough, but only about $800,000 was initially issued, and less than $5000 in actual dollars was put immediately into the Little bank account. Billy needed ready cash for other things. He was heading East.

In the Midwest, betimes, Little was nudging Chevrolet along on the design of two prototypes (one a six, another a four) neither of which would please Durant—"the first . . . from a standpoint of appearance, not satisfactory," he would write, "the second . . . from the standpoint of cost, impossible." Mason was gearing up for engine production. Hardy was trying to find room for a Little

assembly line.

Spring came, then summer, there were no cars—and Billy Durant was in New York announcing yet another new project. He had bought an entire block in Manhattan, 56th to 57th streets on Eleventh Avenue. This was to be the home of the Republic Motor Company, "one of those immense projects which seem essential to Durant's happiness," as *Motor World* put it. And it was, the New York site to be the first of ten projected in the country for the manufacture of motorcars, specifically the Little and the Chevrolet. "Built on the Spot" was to be the Republic slogan. "Grown-up people are very much like children in many respects," Billy Durant would note, "they like to see the wheels go 'round." With Durant's factories scattered throughout the country, potential customers wouldn't have far to travel for a look-see and a soft-sell. But more important, as he told a reporter then, he saw the industry problem not as one of production but one of distribution and "he believes he has solved it."

Of course, he hadn't really seen to the problem of production yet . . . completely. But in late summer the Little Four arrived. It was diminutive and cute. Set on a ninety-inch wheelbase chassis, with integral engine-transmission, its motor was the standard vertical type with cylinders cast in parts, thermosyphon cooling, and a horsepower rating of twenty though, as one admiring reviewer commented, "by reason of large valves and careful workmanship throughout, considerably more power than the rating indicates has been generated without difficulty."

The Little was "simple to the point of innocence," Alex Hardy would confide later, just a tiny motor "revamped and improved by Mason, and put into a small racer for sale at $650." In truth, it was not all that fast, its perky looks probably just making it seem so, nor would it prove very durable. It was "driven to its death in less than 25,000 miles," as Billy Durant later lamented. He had ordered a road test of that duration.

Meantime Louis Chevrolet, if the story be true, had told Billy with delight that he had tested the latest of his prototypes—another six-cylinder—secretly at four one morning on a road outside Detroit, had hit 110 on the way out, was stopped by a road block and an irritated constable on the way back, collared off to jail and upon appearing before the local justice of the peace was fined thirty dollars—five for speeding, twenty-five for impersonating a famous race driver.

Billy was not amused. He thought that was too much, indeed everything about the new Chevrolet was too much. Too big, too heavy, too expensive. But at least he now had something to produce—and he ordered it into production. He also ordered into production a Little Six companion to the Little Four to sell at $1285. He knew he couldn't sell Louis Chevrolet's car for less than $2150.

A new Little was reason enough, in the Durant mind, for another new move—and in September 1912, Billy incorporated the Sterling Motor Company in Michigan as another unit of Republic, which would be devoted initially to the production of six-cylinder engines for the Little (and subsequently the Chevrolet) and which had a similar cast of officer characters as all the other companies thus far put together. In November, when gasoline fuel abruptly came into short supply, Billy Durant got another idea, asked Arthur Mason to design a vehicle to be powered by kerosene, and issued a press release noting the "growing difficulties in the fuel situation" and the wisdom of being "independent of gasoline." But gasoline quickly started flowing again, doubtless there were not enough cars on the road to have created gas lines in any case, and there

---

*in August of 1914 the Chevrolet Motor Company—the "Car" was dropped early from the firm's title—petitioned the Highland Park Council for permission to plat the land for a residential subdivision that would be "one of the most beautiful in the country." This, one news report said, "gives a 'black eye' to the rumor that Ford would buy the land in order to erect a factory for the proposed Ford electric car." Ford did eventually purchase much of the land, but not for the manufacture of an electric car.

was no crisis—so Billy summarily dropped the idea. It was, he probably concluded, as unworthy a notion as his buying of the Cartercar company for General Motors because of its friction drive transmission. Sticking to the mainstream of industry thought was a lot more sensible. He never liked to make the same mistake twice.

Besides, both the Little Six and the Chevrolet were now ready for market. Arriving as they did at the same time was an unfortunate case of bad timing, but Billy Durant didn't feel he should hold back either of them. The Little Four had earned a good initial reception and was selling briskly, and he wanted to capitalize on that success while it was still fresh—and also probably before any of the cars sold to new owners had been driven 25,000 miles. As for the Chevrolet, he simply had to get it out, it had been a year and a half since the first press mention that it was coming.

Officially, it was designed the Chevrolet Six Type C Classic, that imposing title selected as perhaps best fitting the car. It was more formidable than French, scarcely what Durant had had in mind. Its T-head valve-in-head six-cylinder engine had a 3-9/16-inch bore by 5-inch stroke for 299 cubic inches and the largest displacement of any engine Chevrolet would produce until 1958 and the announcement of the 348-cubic-inch V-8. The wheelbase was 120 inches—as long as any Chevrolet ever. And if Louis Chevrolet had indeed hit 110 with it on that road test, the fault was the speedometer's—the Classic Six was ponderous.

This is not to infer that the first Chevrolet was an unmitigated disaster. The motor was supported at three points in the chassis, connecting rods were drop-forged I-beam section with die-cast babbitt bearings, the crankcase was aluminum, camshafts drop forged with cams integral, timing gears were helical type, ignition dual magneto, cooling was by centrifugal pump and fan, lubrication a combination of force-feed and splash. The carburetor was a Stromberg, and starting was initially by an English compressed air system though a Gray & Davis electric starter would be introduced in 1913. (The Chevrolet had electric lighting from the beginning.) A three-speed transmission was mounted on the full-floating rear axle; the front axle was a drop-forged I-beam; steering was worm and gear. There was nothing extraordinary in all this—but it was extremely well put together.

In what perhaps was a reconciliation attempt for reasons of public relations, *Motor World* was invited to send one of its men to Detroit for a personal demonstration of the car by Louis Chevrolet. The reporter came away soundly impressed, and *Motor World* subsequently published the most pleasant commentary it ever had on anything involving Billy Durant.

"Time after time the motor was throttled down so that it barely turned over," the story read, "and with high gear enmeshed the throttle was opened suddenly to the limit without eliciting the usual choking and missing that generally accompanies such practice with a great number of motors. Instead, the motor 'picked up' quickly and steadily, until, at approximately 55 miles an hour, it was necessary to apply the brakes by reason of the threatened activity of the police. Vibration was singularly conspicuous because of its absence. . . . Even at high speed on intermediate gear, the vibration was nil, and the motor was no noisier than it was at 10 miles an hour."

Following this road demonstration, Louis Chevrolet had returned both car and *Motor World* reporter to the factory and provided further evidence of engine smoothness by placing a pencil on the motor and asking the reporter to watch the tach while he revved up to 2000 rpm. The pencil didn't move. All this was possible, he boasted, because of a crankshaft design which kept weight of the reciprocating parts to a minimum and featured integral semi-circular counterweights which "act as supplementary flywheels, in a sense, and insure positive continuity of motion without interruption of balance." All that said, Louis Chevrolet considered his a job well done and bought a ticket on a steamship bound for France and an extended vacation.

Because the Classic Six and the Little Six hit the market at the same time, and because press references invariably mentioned the similarities (including engine) between the two cars, and because one was priced about a thousand dollars less than the other, there was the expected outcome. Billy Durant found himself with two cars, one which could probably be driven forever and which didn't sell, and one the life expectancy of which he already knew was limited and which did sell. Orders for some 3000-odd Littles represented a good beginning, and scant more cash had to be pumped into that operation because checks for deposits paid the overhead. The reported sale of 3000 Chevrolets, on the other hand, was the figmental imagination of someone in a Durant front office somewhere and had nothing whatsoever to do with reality.

The reality was that the Little in Flint was showing a profit and the Chevrolet in Detroit was not. This situation could not long endure—and Billy Durant came up with an obvious solution: the wedding into one of what was good individually about the Little and the Chevrolet—and marketing the result in a price range closer to Ford's. And this new car was to be a Chevrolet. The Little would be discontinued before it had the chance to earn a bad reputation, and also because as Alex Hardy had pointed out, the name itself was a negative that posed problems for salesmen; people generally didn't want to be reminded in capital letters that they were driving a little car even if they were.

Equally logical was the decision to move the Chevrolet operation to Flint, where Durant was worshipped as a wizard, and where Hardy had finally sorted out the old Flint Wagon Works factory and pretty much cleared away all the wagon-making apparatus.

Earlier Durant had planned a different location in Flint for Chevrolet: the former Imperial Wheel plant of Durant-Dort. But that ended abruptly when William C. Durant and J. Dallas Dort parted ways. The reason for the breakup of the Billy-Dallas partnership after more than a quarter of a century was never revealed by either party, and each continued to say very nice things about the other. But now changes were necessary. Durant disassociated himself from all matters Dort, and Dort from all matters Durant. For Billy's part, this meant that the Imperial Wheel factory was no longer available, forcing the relocation to the old wagon works plant. Also necessary was abandonment of the Republic enterprise, in which Dort had been prime backer. Now everything—Republic, Little, Chevrolet—would be gathered together under one banner and it would be called Chevrolet.* Alex Hardy liked that idea by half; he had never cottoned to Republic, that was the name of a truck, he said. He also tried to talk Durant out

*What happened during this short period was midway between a merry-go-round and a game of corporate musical chairs. The Little in essence became the Chevrolet, and the Republic company scheme became in fact the Chevrolet company scheme. The Mason engine-building company, which produced fours, would remain a separate entity for a short period, still under Durant's control. The Sterling engine building company, which produced sixes, was sold to Bill Little who had begun managing that plant after he had

1915 Type H-2 Royal Mail Roadster / Owner: Wayne McKinley

of Chevrolet, but Billy would have none of that. He still loved the name.

And thus did Louis Chevrolet return from his holiday in France to find everything different from the way it had been when he left—and little of it to his liking. He didn't relish at all the idea of his Chevrolet being marketed as a competitor to the Ford. He didn't like the move to Flint. And then there was the smoking incident, which smacks of the apocryphal although both Chevrolet's sister and Durant's widow would confirm it to be true many years later.

Apparently Durant mentioned to Chevrolet that because he was now a motor executive, a switch to more business-like cigars in place of blue-collar cigarettes was in order. Louis hit the ceiling. "I sold you my car and I sold you my name, but I'm not going to sell myself to you," he screamed. According to Catherine Durant, it was not so much Louis' smoking of cigarettes that her husband objected to so much as the way Louis smoked them, the "cigarette hanging on his lower lip . . . it used to annoy Willie to tears." Whatever the specifics, Louis left his car and his name with Durant, and took his cigarettes and himself and got out. Never to return.*

"The policy of this company," subsequent promotion would note, "is to build a good motor car to sell at a reasonable price." In the sorting out which followed, the last units of the Classic Six Chevrolet were run down the line, and for the 1914 model year the Light Six (or Chevrolet Model L) became the successor to the Little Six, although there was production overlap in order to deplete the Little parts on hand. The two cars were quite similar, although the Chevrolet version had a 271-cubic-inch engine that was 51 cubic inches bigger (and also was Chevrolet's only L-head in history), a 112-inch wheelbase that was six inches longer, and a price tag of $1475 which was a couple of hundred dollars more than the Little. The Light Six—which like the Classic Six was available

---

completed his Louis Chevrolet assignment; no argument was involved here, after many years of association with Durant, Little simply felt it was time to strike out on his own, and Billy gave him a good price for Sterling. Etienne Planche, whose assignment with Louis Chevrolet was also finished, was snapped up by J. Dallas Dort, who organized the Dort Motor Car Company in Flint, made Planche its chief engineer, and proceeded to market a motorcar called the Dort, which survived into the Twenties. The old Imperial Wheel plant in Flint was bought in 1914 by R.F. Monroe who organized the Monroe Motor Company to build a $450 runabout with engines supplied by both Mason and Sterling; Billy Durant was a vice-president of the firm, and the Monroe was sold through Chevrolet dealers for several years, until Monroe decided to unfetter himself from Billy's grasp and traded his Chevrolet shares for Durant's Monroe shares—one of history's less astute decisions—and moved to Pontiac. Which left the old Imperial plant idle again, but it was soon sold to Buick. Meanwhile, too, the Monroe company in Pontiac was bought by William Small who moved it back to Flint and who engaged Louis Chevrolet to build a race car, the Monroe-Frontenac which his brother Gaston drove to victory in the 1920 Indy 500. Subsequently the Monroe company ended its life in 1924 under the banner of Premier.

*Louis' temper frequently got the better of him. Reportedly, his fit of pique with Durant led him to dispose of his stock in Chevrolet. Apparently too, he put the kibosh on another potentially lucrative venture in spark plugs during this period when he beat up Albert Champion in the course of a personal argument. Louis was apparently much happier as his own boss. He founded the Frontenac Motor Corporation in 1914. It was sporadically successful, other interim or subsequent Chevrolet adventures not so. After a long illness, he died June 6th, 1941 in Detroit at age sixty-two. He was buried in Indianapolis. In later years he always mentioned as the source of his greatest pride the two Indy 500 winners he designed and built, never the millions of cars which bore his name.

only as a touring car—would be built through the 1915 model season.

More significant certainly for 1914 was the new H series, which introduced a four-cylinder engine whose dimensions (3-11/16 by 4 bore/stroke for 170.9 cubic inches) would remain in Chevrolet production until fours were discontinued in 1928. It was a honey of a unit, designed by Arthur Mason: overhead valves of 1.5 inches, cylinders cast integral with crankcase, removable cylinder head, three-bearing crankshaft, nickel-plated rocker arm cover. Cooling was thermosyphon with fan, lubrication splash with positive pump. The carburetor was Zenith, ignition was by Simms high-tension magneto.

These were the first Chevrolets not to be equipped with a self-starter (an Autolite starter and lighting system was available optionally at $125)—but they were also the first Chevrolets to be sold for under a thousand dollars. And they carried two of the most enchanting model names to grace any motorcars ever: Baby Grand for the touring at $875, Royal Mail for the roadster at $750. And for 1915, when the wheelbase was lengthened two inches (to 106), another delectable offering was provided in the Amesbury Special, what perhaps today might be termed a Decor Package: one-piece folding windshield, lockable watertight rear deck, combination top and dust shield, exposed wooden dash. The Amesbury's price was $985, but usually customers spent an extra $125 for the optional Houk wire wheels. It was a snappy, sporty car.

These new Chevrolets were enormously well received. Said *The Automobile*: "Another instance of the individuality of Chevrolet design is found in the midships location of the gearset, Chevrolet being practically the only inexpensive car to use this design. It is a neatly designed transmission with ball bearings. . . . A distinct feature of Chevrolet cars is their smart appearance, the five-passenger body being of neat outline without going to extremes of fashion."

Though Chevrolet prices were not in the Model T range, nor was production which would double from 5000 to 10,000 in 1915, when Ford topped a half million, Durant was sure he was headed in the right direction. He had the Chevrolet now that he had wanted in the first place, and in 1914 he gave it the emblem he'd been carrying around in his head for some time.

How the bow-tie badge idea got into his head is a source of some conjecture. It was either the motif on the wallpaper of a hotel suite he stayed in during a visit to Paris and he snatched a piece of it and put it in his wallet—which is the way he liked to tell it. Or he spotted it in the rotogravure section of a Sunday newspaper he happened to be reading during a vacation in Hot Springs, Virginia—which is how his widow remembered it. The Paris hotel version was the more romantic of the two, of course—and perhaps is why Billy preferred it, truth notwithstanding. He was obviously very pleased with himself for having thought of it in any case. Some advertisements of late 1914 used only the emblem as illustration, with a legend above it reading, "By this sign ye shall know it."

The tinge of sacrilege that implied was occasionally matched in the text of these advertisements in another vein, with convoluted copy implying that the Chevrolet was a worthy racing competitor to Ralph De Palma's Grand Prix Mercedes, only that car arriving earlier at the finish line in a few Eastern events. "The Chevrolet which finished in second place was built in the New York factory in 29 hours at a cost of less than $1250," one ad burbled. "It beat cars costing nearly ten times that amount."

Apparently these racing Chevrolets were specially prepared—neither their piston displacement of 198 inches nor the $1250 figure matching any car in production. This was perhaps a mini-attempt by Durant to emulate the competition program he had inaugurated at Buick—he always liked racing, his son Cliff became a racing driver of some repute—but it was pursued for only a short while. More important than the Chevrolet performance on the track was the Chevrolet performance in the marketplace, and in challenging in lower-priced field that meant durability and economy. Royal Mail roadsters were sent on numerous reliability runs. And one of them—under the observation of J.E. Schipper of *The Automobile*—was driven round Central Park in Manhattan for 27.9 miles on one measured gallon of gasoline. A cordial invitation was extended in advertisements to visit the factory "in the heart of New York City, four blocks from Broadway."

The factory in the heart of New York City was a mixed blessing. It did provide Billy Durant with a place to show off what he was doing just a stone's throw from Wall Street—and though he was wary of bankers, he knew they were men with a commodity he could always use whenever plans grew grandiose. And they were about to. His factory site, alas, was in an area of town colloquially known as "Murderer's Row"—and he had to buy protection from both the street toughs and Tammany Hall. Billy's offices were initially over a saloon across the street from the plant.

When Billy himself moved to New York, he chose Park Avenue for his home. In 1915 Alex Hardy would rent an apartment in the city as well, since he would now be spending about two-thirds of his time away from Flint. Other moves were being made.

In August of 1914 Durant bought the plant formerly occupied by Maxwell-Briscoe in Tarrytown, New York. He needed money to get it, and he got it—from a New York banker. He had torn up the first leaf which he had decided only a short while before to take out of Henry Ford's book. But buying Tarrytown was the first step in reviving for the Chevrolet company his old Republic company idea of manufacturing plants flung across the country. And he knew just what he wanted to build there: his first head-on competitor to the Model T.

The Chevrolet Four-Ninety was announced on December 16th, 1914, was shown at the New York show beginning New Year's Day, was put into production as soon as the assembly line was ready. Durant wrote a friend: "I am pleased to report as follows; On June 1, 1915, the 'Four-Ninety' was placed on sale. At the close of business June 19, the Chevrolet Motor Company had accepted orders from dealers and distributors—every contract secured by a cash deposit—for 46,611 cars, valued at $23,329,390—a fairly good record for 17 working days. Since June 19, we have orders for more than 1000 cars per day."

He ended the letter with a slogan: "A little child can sell it." There were few adults in America unaware of what 490 meant. It was the price tag of a Model T Ford. Now it was both the designation and the price tag of a Chevrolet.* Six weeks after the Four-Ninety went on sale, the T's price was lowered to $440.

What the Four-Ninety was, in essence, was the Chevrolet stripped to essentials, put on a 102-inch wheelbase and offered in any color so long as it was black. Billy Durant had exchanged one leaf from Henry Ford's book for another. *The Motor*, a British publication, in its favorable critique of the car would offer this interesting rationale: "The finish of the bodywork is in dull black throughout, there being no bright parts to keep clean."

The Four-Ninety's engine was the Model H's, with smaller main and rod bearings, and simplified in bottom-end design and elsewhere to lower manufacturing cost. It developed twenty horsepower, the same as the T. Though never becoming so popular as varied of the Tin Lizzie's foibles, there was a noise made by the Four-Ninety's bevel gear rear axle that some people would begin calling "the Chevrolet hum." No particular nickname apparently was given to the sound made because the rocker arm cover had been taken off.

The designer of the Four-Ninety was Alfred Sturt, again a Buick alum, having served as both test driver and experimental engineer there. He was brought to Chevrolet now at Arthur Mason's suggestion. In addition to his reputation as a mechanical genius, Sturt also had the distinction of installing the first home telephone in Flint.

The Four-Ninety launched, Durant moved again. On July 14th it was announced that Chevrolet in Michigan had acquired the balance of Mason Motor's stock and would begin construction of a new factory capable of producing a thousand engines a day. Billy needed more money, of course, and he returned to the man who had made it possible for him to acquire Tarrytown, the banker Louis Graveret Kaufman, with whom he was beginning to become friendly.

Then he went to see some old friends from his carriage-building days, and was as persuasive as ever. Russell Gardner said he would be delighted to assemble Chevrolets in St. Louis, Missouri—and Norman de Vaux was equally enthusiastic about doing same in Oakland, California, adding that he would be glad to have Billy's son Cliff as a sales executive in the organization. In New York over dinner at Pabst's Restaurant on Columbus Circle, Sam McLaughlin said only two things prevented his building Chevrolets in Canada: lack of space, that area not being used for production of the Buicks that Durant had talked him into years before being devoted to carriages, and his father's possible reluctance to admit the end of the horse-and-carriage era so that the space could be cleared for another automobile assembly line. The elder McLaughlin acceded. And there were Chevrolets in Canada. "Sam McLaughlin says . . . he never saw anything like it," Durant would write soon after. "Chevrolet is the attraction,

---

*It should be mentioned that these prices represent the touring car model for each marque; the Model T roadster was fifty dollars less. And for basal transportation regardless of price, the Model T would unquestionably remain the better bargain for some years. Partly this was because Henry Ford had a head start in producing effectively in quantity, partly it was because of the coming events at Chevrolet. Durant wouldn't be able to hold to the $490 price in any case, though it was a great gimmick for the announcement. Interestingly, at the New York show introduction just two weeks following the preliminary announcement, the price was indicated as $550, but "whenever the company's manufacturing facilities and production justified it, the price on this car, electrically equipped, should be $490." The price of $490 was justified mid-year, by the simple expedient of removing the electrical equipment and offering it as a $60 option. Actually, "offering" is too mild a word. As the brochure said, "We strongly recommend the purchase of the Model Four-Ninety with electric lighting and starting equipment, as no car today is complete without it. If you buy a car without electric lights and starter you will make a mistake." At the beginning of the season following, the self-starter was made standard and the price remained $490, but for not much longer than it took to produce the advertisements for "the lowest priced electrically lighted and started automobile in the market today." Chevrolet simply couldn't make a reasonable profit at $490 with a self-starter, and the company probably felt it was needed as standard on the car just to offer something Ford didn't. The price went back up to $550. Thereafter, generally, as the T's price was lowered, the Four-Ninety's was raised, and the price differential between the two cars widened considerably.

---

and orders and money is being forced upon them in 'chunks'."

Meanwhile someone was beginning to buy large chunks of General Motors stock. And General Motors stockholders were being contacted. Quietly at first. Louis Graveret Kaufman was becoming a better friend of William C. Durant's.

Which of them induced Pierre S. du Pont to join the adventure which followed is in dispute—both would claim the credit. Possibly it was neither. Pierre du Pont himself would remember the instigator being John J. Raskob. Raskob, later to be Al Smith's campaign manager, was treasurer of E.I. du Pont de Nemours and Company, a firm frequently quoted in the press in those days as being "heavily into powder." It was the explosive kind, and du Pont recognized that the fortune he was making in supplying munitions for the war that was raging in Europe was a temporal thing. Even if America became involved—which some considered unlikely at this point—it would not last forever. Raskob was sure the automobile would, that the timidity banking institutions still harbored about the future of the industry was now absurd. What Durant was offering was entrée into a field which offered the brightest of long-range profit possibilities. Kaufman probably acted as the mediator in the du Pont negotiations, and on the side was forming alliances with various GM stockholders who did business with his Chatham and Phenix National Bank.

"Proxies galore with some of the nicest letters you ever read," Billy Durant wrote excitedly as he gathered friends and supporters to the cause. Probably it is true that three days before the General Motors annual meeting, Wilfred Leland of Cadillac visited a gleeful Durant in New York and "he took me into the back office and opened the door of a large safe and showed me a huge stack of stock certificates which he told me would control the outstanding stock of GM." Unfortunately it is not true that on the day of the meeting Durant arrived at the appointed hour followed by assistants carrying bushel baskets of proxies which were ceremoniously set down on the board table as Billy Durant announced, "Gentleman, I now control this company."

That's one legend this writer hates to see die. It's a shame Billy didn't think of it. Doubtless he would have done it if he had. Still, there was an element of drama to it all. Billy Durant had chosen the date of his coup carefully. September 16th, 1915. On the seventh anniversary of the day he founded General Motors, he had it back again.

Congratulations poured in to him. "More power to you," wrote Fred Smith from Lansing. From Flint, Alex Hardy gushed, "I am always yours to command." "You deserve it all and anything more you want," said Arthur Mason.

Billy Durant wanted more. His hold on General Motors was a tenuous one, he knew, born of quickly engineered alliances. His hold at Chevrolet was complete. He spent the following six months preparing another coup.

With Kaufman's assistance, the Chevrolet Motor Company of Delaware was incorporated on September 23rd, which seemed innocent enough, the sole information supplied the press regarding Chevrolet alone, "which will at once expand its manufacturing facilities and contemplates rivaling within another year or two the Ford and Willys-Overland companies, as to output." But the Delaware incorporation was a holding company, capitalized initially at $20 million—which before Christmas was increased to $80 million, with a private, then a published, offer that anyone holding one share of GM stock could trade it for five of Chevrolet. This step was being taken, the press said, for the "acquisition of a controlling interest in General Motors by the Chevrolet company." When it occurred, more than one newspaper carried the headline, "Chevrolet Buys General Motors." Which was a simplification of the machinations but precisely what happened.

The press was as effusive as his friends had been this time. "The master man of the motor world, the genius of the automobile field . . . no man has played a larger part in the progress of the motor car," wrote Richard Spillane in *New York Commerce and Finance.* The *New York Evening Mail* called Durant the peer of Andrew Carnegie and the E.H. Harriman of the motor world. Billy Durant stated it very simply. "I took General Motors back from the bankers today," he said gently to his wife at dinner that night.

What all this meant for Chevrolet had worried a good many people in Flint. Earlier Durant had wired assurance to Alex Hardy: "To set your mind at rest for all time, there is not enough money in this country to buy Chevrolet, or consolidate Chevrolet, or take from our little crowd control of Chevrolet. The Chevrolet is my newest, latest and best Prize Baby dedicated to and controlled by the men who built it up against terrific odds."

Certainly he had kept his promise. General Motors did not engulf Chevrolet. But it did engulf Billy Durant—and he just wouldn't have much time anymore to pay attention to the car which had brought him back to power.

Probably had he given the matter more thought, he would have decided against introducing the Model D V-8 for 1918. As *The Automobile and Automotive Industries* said, with this car "Chevrolet enters a field somewhat different from that in which it has been operating heretofore." In August of 1916 Durant had been forced to "go on record" to categorically deny that the car would be priced at $700, as was being widely published in papers throughout the country. A $700 V-8 would, of course, have been big news. Now, a year later, when a V-8 in the $1400 range arrived, it was not—and the car was poorly received.

This was rather a pity, because although the Chevrolet represented no technological breakthrough, it was an interesting piece of engineering. A 90⁰ V-8 of 3-3/8 by 4-inch bore and stroke, the three-main-bearing unit displaced 288 cubic inches. A patent for the development of its pushrod overhead valves was applied for by Arthur Mason and Alfred Sturt.

The car was set on a wheelbase as long (120 inches) as Louis Chevrolet's Classic Six, and was really a move backward insofar as Durant's strategy for marketing the Chevrolet was concerned. People who bought Royal Mails and Baby Grands couldn't afford it, and people who bought higher-priced cars didn't want it. The Chevrolet V-8 was quietly allowed to die after the 1918 model year.

Meanwhile the rest of the line was moving spectacularly. From sales of 62,522 cars in 1916, Chevrolet more than doubled to 125,004 for 1917. In the latter model year, Chevrolet continued to spell out the designation Four-Ninety, perhaps because the 490 was priced at 550 dollars with the addition of electric starter and lights, and the juxtaposed number figures couldn't be effectively advertised. Added too was an "All-Season" tourer to the previous roadster and touring car, which was a stop-gap until the planned coupé and sedan could be made ready for the following year, at which time various improvements—oil pressure gauge replacing sight feed, water pump replacing thermosyphon, plunger type oil pump replaced by a gear-driven variation, etc.—were added.

The Series H had departed in 1916, replaced for '17 by the Series F, with the same engine but in a wheelbase increased to 108 inches. The Royal Mail and

1917 Model D V-8 Chummy Roadster / Owner: Wayne McKinley

1917 Model D V-8 Touring / Owner: Tom Meleo

1920 Four-Ninety Touring / Owner: Tom Meleo

1920 Model FB 50 Touring / Owners: Tom and Linda Jacobson

Baby Grand names were retained. The F was replaced for '18 by the Series FA which had a longer stroke engine (3-11/16 by 5¼, 224 cubic inches) with water pump replacing thermosyphon and a circulating oil pump, but mounted on the same chassis. The Royal Mail and Baby Grand names were dropped, replaced by Roadster and Touring. The FB followed for '19, with a two-inch increase in wheelbase. The few changes in the model years immediately following were even less noticeable, and the model designation remained the same. The biggest changes were the prices; they were going up.

Obviously nothing much interesting was happening during these years at Chevrolet. Indeed its introduction of a commercial chassis and Chevrolet truck in January 1918 provided the most significant news then—and certainly historically. The company was drifting, steadily improving its industry position, though not even beginning to approach Ford, and seemingly not trying very hard to do that or much of anything else. Even its advertising became lackluster.

There was no excitement. No more were there the meetings in Flint when engineering problems would arise, and tempers would flare, and Billy Durant would end it by saying, "All right, all right, it's a bad situation—we all know that—but what are we going to do about it?" And what needed doing was done. Now the tenor was complacency. From "what are we going to do about it?," the Chevrolet guiding motto seemed to have changed to "how easily can we get by?"

Durant had been the spur in Chevrolet. He had been the leader and the inspiration. He had been the one who wrote enthusiastically after deciding on the Chevrolet that "my next job was to find a car worthy of the name, a car for power, speed, stability, appearance and price that would outclass any other car in the country."

"Some job," he had concluded—and he had only begun it. Now, back at the helm of General Motors, he was on a buying spree.

He had started virtually the moment he was sure that GM was again his. With Kaufman's assistance, he established United Motors, a holding company into which were gathered various automotive supplier firms, among the most notable being Hyatt (which brought Alfred P. Sloan) and Dayton Engineering (which brought Charles F. Kettering) to General Motors. He purchased a sixty percent interest in the Fisher Body Corporation. General Motors Acceptance Corporation was inaugurated, General Motors Export Company was established. He was wheeling and dealing as never before.

But for every peach of a deal, again, there was a lemon. Frigidaire initially looked to be another Heany, but Durant poured money into it, a good deal of it his own—and disaster was averted. There seemed no good reason for adding Sheridan and Scripps-Booth to the GM car lineup, and neither of them would remain on the scene very long. But it was the Samson tractor which proved metaphorically to be Billy Durant's Delilah. The multimillion dollar challenge to the Fordson was a multimillion dollar loss, it sapped Durant's strength, it couldn't have occurred at a worse time.

The recession of 1920 was short, sharp and devastating. And Durant was caught. He was in debt deeper than even he knew. The bankers came back to bail General Motors out.

Billy Durant had made the same mistake twice.

What would become of Chevrolet now?

CHAPTER TWO

CHEVROLET

RESCUING THE CHEVROLET

Copper-Cooled Debacle to First Place Victory

"**Y**ou knew he was grief-stricken," Alfred P. Sloan, Jr. would remember, "but no grief showed in his face. He was smiling pleasantly, as if it were a routine matter . . ."

Billy Durant had lost General Motors.

He had lost Chevrolet. He had lost everything.

"Money? What is money," he said once. "It is only loaned to a man. He comes into the world with nothing, and he leaves with nothing."

On December 1st, 1920, he put on his hat and coat and walked out of the door of General Motors for the last time. When the door closed, a lot of men inside cried. That evening at home, Billy Durant cried too.

Three months later he was expounding to a reporter, "Forget mistakes. Forget failures. Forget everything except what you're going to do now and do it." What he was going to do now was create a new empire, not by buying out Dodge Brothers and Lincoln as rumored, but by beginning again as he had with Chevrolet. Only this time he would call the result Durant Motors. What he was going to do now was demonstrate that not only could he make the same mistake twice, he could do it again too.

Meanwhile, it remained for others to undo what had been done with what was again being called, in historical reference to William Henry Seward and Alaska, Durant's Folly. General Motors was a wreck.

The du Ponts, whom Billy Durant was in large measure responsible for bringing into GM, asked Alfred Sloan what he thought. Again, the responsibility for Sloan's being at GM was Billy's, and it would be largely Sloan's thinking which would prevail in the months ahead. Fortunately, the only decision immediately taken was to change the name of the Durant Building in Detroit to the General Motors Building. A decision discussed being taken would have washed Billy Durant's "best Prize Baby" right out of the corporation.

"It looked tough for Chevrolet," Charles Stewart Mott would recall. Mott was among the various executives looking into and advising upon General Motors matters during these "heartbreaking times." Oakland and Olds were not doing well either (indeed only Buick and Cadillac among all the automobile companies Billy Durant had put together were making any money at all), the demise of Sheridan and Scripps-Booth was being seen to, and now it was about Chevrolet that the darkest talk was heard. In looking at the remaining GM cars and their frequently overlapping price structures, some efficiency experts told Pierre S. du Pont that Chevrolet was a good candidate for oblivion too. Alfred Sloan didn't agree. And while pleading his case, he saw to it that a public relations veneer was glossed upon Chevrolet so the corporation wouldn't appear silly if he won the argument and Chevrolet was saved. The depth of the Chevrolet crisis was never even hinted at in the trade journals.

One of the first things done was to select a replacement for Billy Durant as head of Chevrolet. The announcement was made in the name of Pierre du Pont who was General Motors' new president, a position he would relinquish to Sloan in 1923. The announcement had obviously been drafted by Sloan; it sounded very optimistic—and was accepted in the press as the "token anxiously awaited [from] within the great organization itself and anticipated with interest by the trade at large." Chevrolet's new general manager and president was K.W. Zimmerschied.

Scarcely anyone in Flint knew him, neither did anyone on the west side of Manhattan, or in Tarrytown, or anyplace else where Chevrolets were then being put together. He was a veteran of General Motors, joining the corporation during Durant's first reign, surviving the interim period of Durant's first ouster, remaining during Durant's second reign, surviving Durant's second and irrevocable ouster. Not many in the organization could boast a similar longevity in the recurring face of upheaval. It would appear that it was his apparently implacable nature which made Zimmerschied so ideal for Chevrolet's top post dur-

Alfred P. Sloan, Jr.

ing this period of indecision. But he was selected for other reasons as well. He was not among the coterie of men Billy Durant had brought together to get Chevrolet started and thus did not have the taint of being identified with the company which Billy had used to get General Motors back, and into trouble, once again. His loyalty was to GM, not to Chevrolet. Moreover, he was a "professional metallurgist and engineer of note," and the envisioned advantage of that will be soon apparent; and as assistant to the president of General Motors for two years he had learned to like the mediocre chicken dinners that preceded the after-dinner talks which were an industry requisite, and he had developed

into a "forceful and convincing speaker." This would be helpful as he swung 'round the country and "captured the enthusiasm of the men who are handling the Chevrolet, [he in turn finding] them responsive and ready for the better and bigger business that is in prospect."

The emphasis on the prospective rather than the immediate was unavoidable. For the Chevrolet was not selling. And, likely as not, it would not be a situation quickly to change. April 15th, 1921 saw the removal to Detroit and the Durant-cum-General Motors Building of all production, material, purchasing, traffic, engineering, and production and plant engineering departments of the Chevrolet Motor Company, so the General Motors Corporation could keep a closer hand in. August 13th, 1921 saw the trade press inference "from a semi-official statement this week which was attributed to K.W. Zimmerschied" that Chevrolet models would remain the same for another year. And November 19th, 1921 saw the appointment as Chevrolet chief engineer of Ormond E. Hunt, former chief engineer for the Packard Motor Car Company, subsequently Mercer, and thereafter a short spell in the empire of Emlen S. Hare, one of automotive history's more renowned scoundrels whose contribution to posterity was the effective rendering asunder of three fine American marques, the Locomobile, the Mercer and the Simplex. Hunt's appointment was noteworthy both for the fact of Chevrolet's getting a good man and the fact that he was not a Chevy man. Gradually much of the team Billy Durant had engineered in Flint would be engineered out of the company.

Of these three Chevrolet happenings of '21, probably the only one which most concerned the people selling the car was that they were stuck with the same product. The Chevrolet cried for rehabilitation. But for the Model FB for '22 a switch from Elliot to reverse-Elliot for the front axle, from single- to three-exhaust-port cylinder head, and from insert-type to poured connecting rod bearings which necessitated two-inch longer throws in the crankshaft was the virtual extent of the changes provided. The Four-Ninety's revisions were similarly palliative: emergency brake lever replacing right-hand pedal ratchet, spiral bevel pinion and ring gear replacing straight cut, steering knuckles that were "decidedly more robust." And the cars were sent out the door to be sold.

In lieu of attention to the mechanical ills and quality control which had been plaguing Chevrolet since its initial success had enabled Billy Durant to regain GM and start wheeling and dealing again, there were price cuts—no fewer than three of them during 1921. Price slashing was rampant throughout the industry during this period, particularly in the lower-priced segment of the market because of that man in Dearborn.

During the two years of 1920 and 1921, Model T Ford production doubled (to nearly a million units), while Chevrolet production was halved (to sixty-odd thousand units). Still, had Chevrolet doubled too, there would have remained the blatant reality that Henry Ford was running away with the low-priced field; catching him, for the moment, was impossible, and even trying to was inadvisable. Or as Alfred Sloan said, "it would have been suicidal to compete with him head-on."

Sloan's strategy instead was to take a chunk out of the top of the Model T market, and make it into a price class of its own—low but not lowest, tending to

1922 Four-Ninety Touring / Owner: Don Rumbaugh

the basal but not so abjectly, for a few extra dollars offering more than a five-and-dime, a touch of Tiffany added to a Woolworth product. Thus, it was with chagrin that Sloan noted throughout 1921 references in the American trade press to the Chevrolet price slashes vis-à-vis the Model T, for what he was doing was not an attempt to get the price down to T levels but instead to what had seemed, even to Billy Durant at the outset, to be its natural sales position, though one disregarded in the travail of the years preceding. Thus, too, was Alfred Sloan vexed to note, for example, in a road test from the British magazine *The Motor* a subtitle reading, "The Performance of an Admittedly Cheap American Car"—because it was not Sloan's intention to admit to any such thing.

What Sloan was prepared to admit to—and *Automobile Topics*, at least, acknowledged that "in many ways the two products [Ford and Chevrolet] are not competitors"—was what convinced Pierre S. du Pont to take his advice and not to scrap Chevrolet. In truth, du Pont may have been easy to convince. Because he was hot for air cooling.

Actually the term Chevrolet would use was copper cooling, and it was the idea of Charles F. Kettering, another man brought into GM by Billy Durant. Two weeks prior to the announcement of the appointment of metallurgist Zimmerschied as head of Chevrolet, Kettering had written Pierre du Pont from Dayton that, after two years of experimentation, "the small air-cooled engine of the Ford type is now ready to push toward a production basis." To du Pont, this was one terrific way to arrive at the upper-echelon/lower-priced car that Sloan was arguing the Chevrolet should be—a Model T competitor with a difference.

Everyone on the new General Motors Executive Committee, which had been instituted in order to prevent rash decisions of the one-man-rule Durant regime, thought it was a nifty idea too. Unfortunately the Executive Committee was composed of individuals who knew a lot about finance and administration but not a good deal about cars. They assumed Zimmerschied would turn cartwheels over the air-cooled engine, and when the metallurgist didn't, they wondered why: Kettering thought it was "the greatest thing that has ever been produced in the automobile world"—and Kettering, after all, had come up with the self-starter. Zimmerschied said he was already coming up with an improved Chevrolet Four-Ninety; the Executive Committee was unimpressed, and replied that he should prepare for the air-cooled engine as "the adopted standard." Zimmerschied mentioned something about lines of responsibility but no one paid much attention. Kettering was worried that Zimmerschied's apprehension would result in the design from Dayton being changed at Chevrolet in Detroit, and was delighted when the Executive Committee decided that an air-cooled six was an admirable idea too, because Oakland's general manager George H. Hannum was as gung-ho copper-cooling as Kettering himself. By now Alfred Sloan began having doubts. But Pierre du Pont said he felt "like a small boy when the long ex-pected circus posters begin to appear on the fences." It was an appropriate analogy. Copper-cooling was a three-ring affair.

The first Dayton-built cars were to be introduced at the New York Automobile Show in January 1922, with production to begin at Oakland in Pontiac the following month, and Chevrolet thereafter, once its splendid success provided a told-you-so to the still reluctant Zimmerschied. Things didn't happen that way.

Instead the first air-cooled six arrived in Pontiac from Dayton for testing—

1923 Superior Series B Tou

ner: Charlie Shannep

1923 Copper-Cooled Chevrolet / Henry Ford Museum & Greenfield Village

1923 Superior Series B Four-Door Sedan / Owner: George Templin

and performed so miserably that Hannum, while still enthusiastic in principle, decided that a lot more practice was needed and that "to bridge the time . . . we are planning on bringing in a complete new [water-cooled Oakland] line . . ." This so unnerved the super-sensitive Kettering that the Executive Committee sent him a letter personally signed by each of its members—du Pont, Sloan, John Raskob and J.A. Haskell—as well as by Charles Stewart Mott, who was group executive for the car divisions, noting that "it is quite natural that there should be a lot of 'wiseacres' and 'know-it-alls' standing around knocking the development"—and thereafter decided to throw the program back at one of them.

Zimmerschied was aghast. What a Christmas present this was. It was December 15th, 1921. The air-cooled Chevrolets were scheduled for production September 1st, 1922.

The hope was that the four would succeed where the six had failed, and to better the odds, Ormond E. Hunt and the chief engineers of Oakland and Buick were sent to Dayton to help out. Sloan by now was having increasing doubts. He investigated a steam-cooling system with Zimmerschied which turned out not to be a viable alternative but, more important, convinced the Executive Committee that a dual water-cooled/air-cooled program should be implemented for Chevrolet, just in case . . .

Zimmerschied breathed a little easier. For a little while. But on February 22nd, 1922, Charles Stewart Mott had hired as his manufacturing assistant a brilliant young executive who had served very ably as production manager at Ford until his continuing differences with Henry resulted in his taking leave of the company in what by then had become a Dearborn tradition. He was fired. And he quit.

Once at GM, William S. Knudsen was immediately despatched to Dayton. On March 11th, he recommended enthusiastically and personally to Pierre du Pont "that the car be put into production at once." To Sloan, he advised what he meant was production on an experimental basis—but the endorsement of a former Model T man for a Chevrolet project was all that du Pont wanted to hear. "And then there was a break-up in the Chevrolet organization," as Charles Stewart Mott remembered it.

Actually it was a breakdown, and Zimmerschied had it. Whether it was a complete nervous collapse is not known, but it provided the public relations convenience of informing the press that the management shift was the result "of the expansion of the [Chevrolet] business, which has grown too big to be humanly possible to be handled in detail by one man." Knudsen was named vice-president of operations for Chevrolet; K.T. Keller would be retained as manufacturing manager, a position he had assumed during the Durant era and would keep until he decided to cast his fortunes with Walter Chrysler in 1926. The general managership of Chevrolet was removed from Zimmerschied—Pierre du Pont said he wanted it himself—but the presidency of Chevrolet remained his, and he now also had the title of assistant to the president of General Motors which of course was what he had been before Chevrolet. Zimmerschied was not so distraught to fail to recognize what all this meant. He decided to give his wounded psyche a rest—and retired.

Meantime Olds joined in the copper-cooling caper, and the reader is asked to forgive the precious alliteration but a caper is just what it all now was. Internal memos began flying like kites in a gale storm, there was no direction. And there

1924 Superior Series F Two-Passenger Coupe / Owner: Scott M. Schondelmyer

1924 Superior Series F Touring / Owner: Robert D. Mergy

was also no air-cooled engine. By November there was, and it was accompanied by an Executive Committee directive to Chevrolet "to proceed . . . cautiously, in such a way that the hazard to the Corporation is at all times kept at a minimum." A month later, as automobile show time rolled 'round, GM spokesmen were equally cautious in talking to journalists. The car had been widely bruited throughout its development period. Now *Automotive Industries* reported, "It is no longer experimental in any engineering sense, it simply remains to be seen whether its advantages offset its abnormality enough to create a lasting demand on an adequate scale." *Automobile Topics* said, "it is understood that no active selling campaign will be undertaken immediately."

The copper-cooled Chevrolet was a smash hit at the automobile show. It was a disaster everywhere else. According to Alfred Sloan, 759 of the cars were produced; 239 of them were scrapped in production; 20 got lost someplace; the remaining 500 were dispatched to the sales organization, of which 150 were used by factory representatives, over 300 were assigned to dealers, and about 100 found actual buyers. In June 1923 Chevrolet decided to recall them all. Two are known to exist today: the one in Harrah's Automobile Collection had been sold to a Boston man who refused to give it back; the other, in Greenfield Village, had been bought by Henry Ford who wanted to see what all the fuss was about.

The fuss was about an engine which promised to have fewer parts, less weight, lower cost and higher performance than a water-cooled unit. It was Kettering's discovery of a unique method of fusing copper to iron at 1400°F which had fired him up on the idea. He had misfired, so did his engine—and that was its principal problem. "The action is like ex-President Wilson's vicious spiral in the cost of living," GM engineer H.D. Church would report. "The higher the temperatures, the worse the detonation and the higher the temperatures." The engine's centrifugal fan drew air up over the cylinders by suction, the warmest air passing over the top of the heads which were not provided the copper cooling fins. This unevenness of cooling air flow combined with low-grade gasoline and even a relatively modest 4.0 to one compression ratio for the continuing pre-ignition problem.

That Sloan was relieved to forget the whole copper-cooling episode was demonstrated in the letter he wrote after Kettering received the "staggering blow" of its abandonment. Very nicely, he suggested that if Kettering was anxious to continue, perhaps a little facility could be set up in Dayton for an "operation . . . of a specialty nature." He knew Kettering was no manufacturing man, and the idea went nowhere. "It just died out," he wrote impishly in his memoirs. "I don't know why."

As for Kettering, he never admitted failure. At a meeting of the Society of Automotive Engineers in the mid-Twenties, when asked why Chevrolet dropped air cooling, his response was "the development of crankcase ventilation made it unnecessary." He didn't talk about it much after that, and went on to research in high octane gasolines and high compression engines, among other areas in which he would enjoy considerable success.

The copper-cooled car was interesting in Chevrolet's history for reasons other than the contretemps surrounding it. It had 3½-inch-square bore/stroke dimensions, a novelty then, and its 135 cubic inches was the smallest displacement engine in Chevrolet history. (It developed a humble 20 bhp at 1750 rpm.) Unique to a Chevrolet motorcar product then, and in some cases ever, were its driveshaft emergency brake, multiple disc clutch, vertically-mounted starter, 37

1925 Superior Series K Touring / Owner: Len Reseck

automatic spark advance, and one-piece semi-floating rear axle. Its price was a variance too, and an unpleasant one; at $725, it was $200 more than the production Chevrolet with which it shared most other specifications.

That in itself was anathema to Sloan, and he wrote off the entire copper-cooling saga as an excellent object lesson in the need to make "an effective distinction between divisional and corporate functions in engineering, and also between advanced product engineering and long-range research." Even Pierre du Pont tended to agree.*

Fortunately, there had been other cars for Chevrolet to sell as this painful lesson was being learned. Chevrolet called them Superior. They were, as Zimmerschied had said, the Four-Ninety made better, but offered at the same price: $525 for the touring car.

Introduced a month and a half before the copper-cooled Chevrolet, the Superior reflected the direction in which Sloan wanted Chevrolet to travel. It was on a wheelbase one-inch longer (103 inches) than the Four-Ninety, and the Four-Ninety's larger companion car, the Model FB, was dropped as encroaching upon Oakland and Olds territory and obfuscating the territory Sloan wanted carved out of the Model T terrain for Chevrolet. Its higher radiator and straight-line hood, more deeply crowned fenders and new drum-type headlamps were modishly in keeping with the contemporary body design for virtually all cars in America except the Model T Ford. Debuting for '23 as the Series B, the Superior would be continued for '24 as the Series F with the Sedanette being replaced by a four-passenger coupé and coach, and the addition of three body styles (touring, coupé and sedan) called DeLuxe and so equipped. A radio by Westinghouse had even been offered awhile the year previous: "This layout makes use of the 6-volt storage battery already a part of the car's equipment," the trade press said. "With it, broadcasted matter may be heard within a radius of 100 miles from the transmitting station. Concerts may even be heard while the car is in motion, though interference from the ignition system of the engine is somewhat objectionable." Because the radio's $200 price tag was about a quarter that of the car, Chevrolet didn't expect to sell many. But it made for an offbeat promotion.

The general promotion was strictly to the point. "The World's Lowest Priced *Quality* Automobile," the ads said. "Unequaled in Style, Value and Economy. . . . Nothing Compares with Chevrolet."

Comparisons are odious, as virtually every literary figure in the Fourteenth Century tried to say first, so it's perhaps best simply to recount what Chevrolet did. In retrospect, it's amazing that dissolution of the company had been contemplated because, once promoted, even the unrehabilitated Chevrolet of '22 had begun selling. In March that year *Automobile Topics* noted in an overall survey of General Motors' lines that "Chevrolet, which serves the fast-growing quantity market, is doing remarkably well, and is believed to have been quietly developing a degree of strength which is pretty generally unsuspected." In November the magazine allowed that what it had suspected all along was now reality. From a production of sixty-odd thousand in calendar '21, Chevrolet was heading toward a 250,000 year for '22. The exact figure was 242,373—and it

*Although his acquiescence was not nearly so important now. He had just retired from GM—his tenure had from the outset been planned as interim—to spend more time with the other du Ponts in Delaware.

would nearly double in '23 to 483,310.

On February 22nd, 1923, the one-millionth Chevrolet was produced. "The fact that the millionth car was turned out on Washington's birthday was only a coincidence," the press commented. In fact, Chevrolet hadn't even noticed, plant executives discovering several thousand cars later in totting up the figures that the mark had been passed. *Automotive Industries* observed that under "ordinary business conditions the holiday might have been observed with suspension of manufacture in honor of Washington." There was no time for that, obviously. By now there had been time to convert the former Janesville (Wisconsin) home of the ill-fated Samson tractor to Chevrolet assembly, further assembly plants were readied in Ohio (Norwood) and New York (Buffalo) and at home in Michigan Chevrolet began taking over the manufacture itself of hundreds of small and large components previously purchased outside.

On January 15th, 1924, William S. Knudsen, who had long since cooled on the Kettering project and was going full bore for Chevrolet, was named the division's president and general manager. During this interim period, there had been some jostling about among general sales managers, but now Richard H. Grant settled himself solidly in that position.

Knudsen had gone to Sloan to ask if there was someone in General Motors he could have. "Dick Grant, who is with Delco Light," Sloan replied. "You can have him." Grant was then Delco's general manager, but he "is essentially a salesman," Sloan said. He couldn't have made a better recommendation. Grant was a full head shorter than Knudsen, but he had tall ideas. As tall as Knudsen's. At a dealer meeting at the Palmer House in Chicago, soon after his appointment, Grant cajoled Knudsen into saying a few words. That's what he asked for, and that's what he got. Incredibly nervous, Knudsen stood up upon being introduced, stuck his arms straight up in the air with index fingers pointed, and in a shaky voice to which the Danish accent he thought he had lost years before suddenly returned, he shouted, "I vant vun for vun." And abruptly sat down. After a few minutes of whispering in the audience, everyone figured out he meant a Chevrolet for every Ford. But even he knew that was unlikely just yet.

Both Knudsen and Grant took the time on November 3rd, 1924 to celebrate Chevrolet's thirteenth birthday with a party and a long press release recounting the company's history and particularly its "phenomenal growth" of the three years past. There was a reason: a gingerly juggling of the figures. Thus, it could be said that "more than 1,000,000 Chevrolets have been produced since January 1st, 1922," without mentioning that one-quarter of them had arrived the first year, one-half the second, and one-quarter the third. Chevrolet was backsliding. There was a reason for that too.

For the 1924 model year, Chevrolet had issued a handbill noting its superiority over "our nearest competitor"—i.e., standard gear transmission versus planetary, water pump versus thermosyphon, 103-inch wheelbase versus 100, oil gauge on dash and Alemite system versus splash lubrication, Remy ignition versus spark coil and timer, rear-mounted gas tank versus under-seat location, four springs versus two, a foot accelerator versus hand throttle. That's what the Chevy had that looked better than the Ford. But the Chevy had other things not so good.

Among them, "it had [that] infamous rear end," as Alfred Sloan called it in his memoirs. "But there is no use specifying its deficiencies." It was Sloan's belief that the "retarded development of Chevrolet's design during the previous

three years" was responsible for the slump of '24, and certainly the copper-cooling distraction was in turn responsible in large measure for the retarded development. Actually, Chevrolet should have waited until '25 to call its car Superior. Because then it was.

Instead it was designated, for no logical alphabetical reason, the Series K. It still had a 103-inch wheelbase. It still had the sturdy 3-11/16-by-4-inch, 171-cubic-inch four. But that was about it. "This job, sprung on the trade without any announcement of price, created somewhat of a stir," *Automobile Topics* said. "There is hardly a feature of the Chevrolet that is not new, improved or redesigned, while most of these features are of the type and quality characteristic of higher priced cars." Ormond Hunt and crew had done well. When the prices were revealed, they were but fifteen to seventy-five dollars more than the year previous—for a whole lot more car.

In the engine, cylinder block, connecting rods and crankshaft were new. Rocker arms were enclosed, and automatically lubricated by thick felt pads saturated with oil. The larger crankshaft had twenty percent greater bearing surface, its cheeks were much heavier. Pistons had scraper rings with relief oil holes at the lower grooves, piston pins were now lapped after the finish grinding operation. A shorter intake manifold brought the carburetor closer to the engine for better carburetion and easier starting.

The channel steel frame was longer and stronger, with five cross members instead of four. And the "Chevrolet hum" would be heard no more. The "infamous" rear end of the Chevy was gone. The legacy of the copper-cooled car was more than confusion; the new rear axle was the one-piece banjo-type developed for it, with the entire differential mechanism mounted in a carrier which included the torque tube, and described now as "similar in design and construction to that used on the most costly cars." The utilization of vanadium steel was increased throughout. There were semi-elliptics all around; they had been arduously tested in day-night driving over bumpy roads for many thousands of miles, the drivers being ordered to "bust those springs if you can." They couldn't.

A dry plate disc clutch completely enclosed with flywheel replaced the former cone. Brake drums were increased from ten to eleven inches in diameter. The worm and wheel steering gear and its supporting bracket were strengthened, so was the transmission and universal joint. The horn button was placed in the center of the steering wheel, a dashlight was standard. The former enameled steel radiator shell gave way to duralumin, what Chevrolet called a "new rustless airplane metal." Closed bodies had a one-piece "Vision Ventilation" windshield. All bodies had new colors; Chevrolet was the first low-priced car to go Duco. One couldn't get a Chevy in any color so long as it was black; indeed, black didn't even appear on its charts, though it was the color for the shiny fenders. Standard body color for the touring, roadster and coach was a rich, dark blue; for the sedan, aquamarine; for the coupé, sage green.

Chevrolet built over a half million cars in 1925.

If the K in Superior K Series should in justice have designated anything, it was Knudsen. He was the one man most responsible for the Chevrolet turnaround. Sloan had the idea, Knudsen made it work. And did he work. Most subordinates called him Mr. Knudsen, but he signed himself simply Knudsen, or just a K with a ring around it, it took less time that way.

His entrance on the Chevrolet scene had been a sticky one. In the turmoil of

1925 Superior Series K Pick-Up, wood body by Hercules Corporation / Owner: Albert Johnson

41

Durant's ouster, and the shakeup of personnel that followed, any new man was regarded with suspicion. During Knudsen's first day on the job, a department head had called to request an appointment. "When you want to see me," he replied, "you open the door and walk in and sit down." The man arrived, shaking visibly. Knudsen told him to go back to his office and calm down. "And while you're at it," he added, "just pass the word around that I'm not bringing any Ford men here to take your jobs."

His job was to compete with the man whose employ he had left under bitter circumstances, and it was one he relished. He had a consuming ambition to beat Ford, on Chevrolet's terms, though he insisted he carried no grudge. But he went about his job with an affable fury.

"I've never stood on the dignity of my position," he would say later, when he rose to the presidency of General Motors. "The fact is, I detest it." At Chevrolet he could be seen frequently in the plant, picking up a rivet gun and demonstrating to the workers how to drive rivets faster. He didn't like paperwork, nor reports or memoranda more than a page long. His desk was generally clear, save for a few loose-leaf books full of charts and field reports that told him where he stood. He wrote all his letters in longhand on a legal-size yellow pad: "When you write it out yourself," he explained, "you don't say too much." The letters were then typed by a male secretary; he refused to have female secretaries because he didn't want to be rude, and he didn't want to give up swearing. He hated the telephone, and buzzers even more; he frequently delivered a memo to a subordinate in person.

He was a big man, and once a year he would pile into a little Chevy and, with Richard Grant beside him, tour the dealerships selling his car. They made it to forty-seven states in all, never to Florida curiously, though perhaps they feared they would be distracted by its booming resort atmosphere. At every showroom, they asked what was wrong with the Chevrolet, and their breezy "hi guys" approach meant dealers weren't inhibited in responding. The list of defects, therefore, was a long one. Not everything noted was attended to, but when most dealers complained, it was.

Attended to as well was the matter of the two-millionth Chevrolet, an episode amusing to research in retrospect. One can envision the office scene, department heads reminding themselves daily that they'd best not let this one slip by too. On January 17th, 1925 a press release was issued with the headline, "Chevrolet Prepares for 2,000,000th Car." It was a bit premature, since the story which followed indicated that if the present schedule was adhered to the car would arrive some time that summer. As it happened, the car was built on September 8th. Chevrolet was "the second company in the automobile industry" and "the first maker of selective gearshift cars" to reach the two-million level. Knudsen preferred the latter designation; he liked the idea of being first. The 50,000 unsolicited testimonials from Chevy owners received in '25 would be advertised as "the greatest collection of complimentary letters ever received in one year by any automobile company." The record-setting two-millionth Chevrolet, a coach, was sent around the country for exhibition.

And William Knudsen set sail for Europe to drum up business over there. Chevrolets had been marketed (and later assembled) overseas in relatively modest numbers for some years; Knudsen returned to the States in December saying that 80,000 Chevies would be sold in Europe in '25, triple the figure for '24, and he expected a 100 percent increase over that for '26. Meanwhile Richard

1926 Superior Series V Roadster / Owner: Paul A. Spies

44   *1926 Superior Series V Touring / Owners: John Motte & Sons*

Grant stayed home and, with ad manager J.E. Grimm, Jr. and the advertising agency of Campbell-Ewald, worked up a plan to coordinate dealer and factory in national and local promotion. Earlier in '25 Grant had been joyed to discover that the new Chevrolets were "purchased from specifications and photographs only." The cars could be purchased from good ads too. Hopefully the factory people would catch up to the demand soon. They were trying hard enough.

In August the Chevrolet sported a heavy front tie-bar which, the company said, "permits better mounting of lamps and affords a convenient place to hang the license plate"—and also made for a production convenience since the previous fender mounting had necessitated two different lamps for the right and left sides. The spark and throttle controls were removed from the steering column to the dash, and the steering wheel was now solid walnut with notched finger grip. The radiator and engine splash pans were strengthened, and there were new colors and upholstery. These running improvements were casually announced, a week after closed car prices were reduced from forty to fifty dollars.

This same effective tactic was used the following January when the '26 Superior V Series was announced: a price reduction of fifteen to fifty dollars first, followed by a rundown of how much more the Chevrolet purchaser would receive for less. In this case the improvements included lighter reciprocating parts via adoption of a "skeleton" piston and new connecting rod design, three-point motor suspension, a belt-driven generator "used on many popular high-priced cars today" in place of the former gear-driven type, an increase of one-third in the surface area of the service brake, removal of the oil pump from behind the generator to the crankcase where it was driven by spiral gears off the camshaft, the generator now belt driven from the crankshaft. A landau sedan at $865, "the most pretentious offering yet mounted on the present style chassis," was added, and variations of gray were the "improved colors," designated gun metal, Bloomfield and Arizona—and there was a new blue called Algerian. Late V Series cars had stoplamp combined with taillight, a running change added when it was decided to return the spark and throttle controls to the steering wheel.

This practice of running in changes when they were deemed advisable for reasons of production and announcing them when effective for reasons of promotion was one which suited Chevrolet engineers and managers just fine. But at the corporate level, there was a round-robin discussion chaired by Alfred Sloan, including the general sales managers of the various GM divisions, and revolving around the question of yearly models. The transcript makes interesting reading, because the consensus after all the banter was that General Motors did not, nor should it, have annual models. And, of course, it did. Particularly Chevrolet, because as Alfred Sloan put it so succinctly, "We expected Ford, generally speaking, to stay put."

That Ford was doing exactly that was cause for considerable consternation in Dearborn. As the months passed, it grew to near paranoia, especially when in 1926 a highly valued dealer in Buffalo said he was giving up his Ford franchise to take on Chevrolet, could not be persuaded otherwise, and his action was the beginning of a trend. "Every day this sort of information comes in here by the bushel," Charles Sorensen cried in exasperation one morning when he opened another letter with another clipping, another Ford defection, another Chevrolet production record. Model T owners were writing in by the hundreds, berating the Tin Lizzie, demanding a new car. When apprised of such things, Henry Ford

1927 Capitol Series AA Touring / Owner: Verl Newman

1927 Capitol Series AA Coach / Owner: Dean Rumbaugh

45

1927 Capitol Series AA Depot Wagon / Owner: Calvin Jordan, Jr.

muttered, "Is that what they're saying?"

In May of 1926 Knudsen announced a $10 million expansion program—the largest in Chevrolet's history thus far—because he wanted to be "ready to produce a million cars in the coming year." In late December it was revealed that in '26 Chevrolet had sold 692,000 cars, Ford 1,550,000. Chevrolet's figure represented an increase of 200,000 over 1925, Ford's a loss of a half million. In Detroit A.W.L. "Doc" Gilpin joined C.E. Dawson and Harry J. Klingler as assistant sales managers for Chevrolet. Richard Grant needed all the help he could get. In Dearborn clippings poured in from news services with headlines like "Ford Cuts Price to Meet Competition." It was incredible. Ford had been cutting prices routinely since the First World War. But never to meet the competition. Ford had had no competition.

In the history of advertising perhaps there has never been an easier job than the one Campbell-Ewald had in 1927: selling the new Chevrolet. Chevrolet had cut its prices too. And come up with "The Most Beautiful Chevrolet in Chevrolet History." Some ads showed the car. Others just pictured a peacock with feathers unfurled. The new bodies had a double belt, full crown fenders, a revised radiator shell and bullet-shaped headlamps. In the new $715 sport cabriolet, Chevrolet also had the first rumble seat in any American low-priced car, and mid-season the Imperial landau replaced the former landau sedan, still with landau irons but no rear quarter windows this time. The cars were now called Capitol instead of Superior.

There wasn't much really new otherwise—rectangular brake and clutch pedals instead of oval, a new release grip and position for the parking brake, a dash-mounted ignition/steering lock, an AC air cleaner and oil filter, disc wheels and balloon tires standard throughout the line. But it was enough.

During the second week of January 1927, William Knudsen drove the three-millionth Chevrolet off the assembly line in Flint, and in Chicago the biggest neon sign west of New York City (8564 bulbs of 10, 20 and 25 watts, and three flashes) provided passersby near Michigan and Randolph "radiating waves of light," the correct time, and a few well-chosen words about Chevrolet.

During the second week of February 1927, *Automobile Topics* juxtaposed two headlines. "Chevrolet Shatters All January Records," said one. "Ford Says Engineers Are Building New Car," said the other.

In early April, "Down-East Yankee" Richard Grant—as *Motor West* called him—was speaking to his dealers on the Pacific Coast, swearing "as wholesomely as a Westerner of the wide open spaces," and talking of "numbers and sums nothing short of millions." In late April, in a review of the industry year to date, *Automobile Topics* noted, "Chevrolet, with its twelve great factories running night and day and an enormous advertising and selling campaign, speaks for itself."

In May 1927 there was silence in Dearborn. As Alfred Sloan remarked, "not many observers expected so catastrophic and almost whimsical a fall as Mr. Ford chose to take . . . when he shut down his great River Rouge plant completely . . . to retool."

William Knudsen had won. Chevrolet had become the largest producer of motorcars in the United States of America. Even by default it felt mighty good. But whether it would last was anyone's guess. Knudsen had worked for Henry Ford. He didn't know what to expect next. Neither did anyone else.

CHAPTER THREE

CHEVY GOES SIX

The Arrival of the Cast Iron Wonder

The Model A Ford arrived on December 2nd, 1927. Two million dollars in advertising accompanied it, at least twenty-five million people saw it that first week at automobile shows and Ford showrooms. It created a furor that was unprecedented in the history of the American automotive industry. It had sprightly styling, a standard transmission, a 103½-inch wheelbase, four-wheel mechanical brakes—and a four-cylinder engine.

There had been no question in William Knudsen's mind since the Ford shutdown in May of '27 that Henry Ford and what he was going to do would be the focus of national attention for the remainder of the year. Nor that the car to replace the Model T would effectively steal the thunder from whatever Chevrolet might introduce at the same time. Henry Ford was a national folk hero; Chevrolet was by contrast an upstart. Thus Knudsen spent much of 1927 reading the newspapers about Ford, getting his Chevrolet house in order, and building as many cars as he could. With Ford operations halted, obviously he could sell every Chevrolet he made. He made over a million of them.

In June of '27 Richard Grant had been promoted to vice-president of sales, Harry Klingler became general sales manager, and the Chevrolet sales staff was strengthened for the battle ahead. In October, Chevrolet staged its second annual "turkey-bean" sales contest among its 27,000 salesmen, with banquets organized throughout the country, winners getting the bird, losers dining only on beans and obliged to pick up the tab for the entire repast. In December, fifteen days after the debut of the Model A Ford, at the Hotel Roosevelt in New York, the Chevrolet for 1928 was introduced. It was designated the National.

Like the Model T, it had four-wheel brakes. Horsepower of its 171-cubic-inch four was up 11.5 percent (35 hp vis-à-vis the Model A's 40), this by an increase in valve diameter and lift, enlargement of the intake manifold and carburetor jets, the compression ratio raised from 4.3 to 4.5 to one, and such refinements as adoption of mushroom type valve tappets, invar strut alloy pistons, and a two-port exhaust manifold replacing the old single port. The car's wheelbase was increased from 103 to 107 inches. Like the Model T, the Chevrolet was attractively styled. Edsel Ford had been largely responsible for the pleasant look of the Model A, Harley Earl for the look of the new Chevrolet. It had been Knudsen's decision—and a wise one—to enlist the help of the head of General Motors' newly-created Art and Colour Section. Commenting that the Chevrolet's "long, sleek hood greatly enhances the appearance of the whole car," *MoToR* added it was "interesting to note" that all four inches of the increased wheelbase had been put in front. What the 1928 Chevrolet didn't have was what those four extra inches were for: a six-cylinder engine.

In January of 1928 in Flint, Chevrolet produced its four-millionth automobile. In February in Dearborn, only 130 Model A's were leaving the assembly line each day. Henry Ford was having production problems, they continued through the spring. Knudsen had another Chevrolet assembly line going in Atlanta, construction on yet another was being rushed in Kansas City. In August Knudsen and Grant took off on their annual trek of the dealerships, arranging to be back in Flint on September 4th when the one-millionth Chevrolet built since the day after New Year's came off the line. Reporters computed that a new Chevrolet was being built every ten seconds of every working day, a million cars in a little more than 200 days divided to five thousand Chevrolets a day. It would be November before Ford would reach a 6000-a-day output. Inexorably, Chevrolet was making itself capable of a mass production equal to Ford's. Because of Ford's early Model A assembly line difficulties—

William S. Knudsen

unexpected in the industry, a pleasant surprise for Knudsen—Chevrolet stayed ahead of Ford in the sales race. The "1st Choice of the Nation for 1928," Campbell-Ewald ads declared that summer. "In 1928, Again the World's Largest Builder of Automobiles" that December. But now Ford was swinging

into full production.

Unmistakably, Chevrolet could have had a six in 1928; the smaller four in the car, indeed, made a fan shroud necessary up front for effective low-speed cooling, though it was the rare reporter who noticed or wondered why—in print anyway. The engine was ready. It was delayed pending the Model A's arrival and allowing for an interval thereafter so the really new Chevrolet could command center stage all by itself. It was a very smart thing to do.

Chevrolet had prepared well for the launching of a six, although the project initially was a corporate one. A market-price graph Alfred Sloan had requested early on for all General Motors cars indicated a gap just above Chevrolet and below Olds. It should be filled with a "Chevrolet chassis with a six-cylinder engine," Sloan concluded—and Henry M. Crane who had designed the fine, if short-lived, six-cylinder Crane-Simplex and was now an engineering consultant to Sloan, had proposed a short-stroke, L-head six. What the car would be had not yet been decided, although some parameters had. It would not be a Chevrolet, it would not be a low-priced economy car; it would instead be a popular-priced car with economy advantages.

Unfortunately, as Sloan wrote to Oakland general manager George Hannum on November 12th, 1924: "Every time it comes up some one wants to make something different and the result of that is that if everybody had their way we would have a second Olds or probably an Oakland car, more likely a second Buick or Cadillac . . . . Therefore, I have been discussing the matter with Mr. Knudsen and feel that we should turn over to Mr. O.E. Hunt, his Engineer, all that we have accomplished, let him weigh it carefully, let him undertake to work out for us a six-cylinder engine along constructive lines, recognizing, as he does, what the picture has got to be. As a matter of fact, Chevrolet should be experimenting with engine developments on its own account and these two things should work along concurrently . . . ."

Thus it was that Chevrolet began development of the project which ultimately was turned over to Oakland and resulted in the car called Pontiac. Valuable experience in six-cylinder engine design had been gained by Chevrolet and when, a couple of years later, Knudsen was aware that a new car would have to be forthcoming soon from Ford and that Chevrolet could not expect to hold its advantage with the car it then had, Chevrolet Engineering was ready to meet the assignment.

The decision for a Chevrolet six was characteristically settled upon. At a meeting when arguments for continuation of a four were pressed, Knudsen listened politely for a few minutes, then stood up and said, "Gentleman, we make a six"—and walked out. Tarrying on decisions was never the Knudsen way. At another meeting when grooves for a new Chevrolet steering wheel became the subject of boring debate, Knudsen picked up the wheel, walked 'round the table, whispered to everyone sitting there, returned to his chair and said, "Gentlemen, we have grooves."

He got the Chevrolet six-cylinder engine into production with equal facility. By introducing the longer chassis for 1928, he had effectively divided his tooling by about half. He only had the engine to worry about for '29. As he later explained: "While the main plant at Flint was still turning out four-cylinder cars,   *49*

1928 National Series AB Coupe / Owner: Thomas G. Coates

at a branch factory in another city, in Saginaw, I put up an assembly line for six-cylinder engines. When we got ready to manufacture, I picked it up bag and baggage and moved it to Flint. Then I shut off the four-cylinder assembly line and put on the six-cylinder line. It was easy. Anybody could do it."

He made no mention of the man who hadn't been able to do it. Conversion to the Chevrolet six had taken Knudsen forty-five days. Ford had required the better part of a year for his Model A.

The Chevrolet six was introduced a few days before Thanksgiving. On the evening of December 25th, Knudsen received a telephone call at home. It was Henry Ford wishing him a Merry Christmas. The following conversation took place:

"You can have a Model A, if you want it."

"Thank you, Mr. Ford, but I have one running at the proving ground and it is running all right."

"That's fine, William. Glad to hear it. You can have anything you want from us."

Later, through the grapevine, Knudsen learned that Henry Ford wanted to see him to entice him back to the Ford Motor Company. Knudsen made no attempt to confirm the rumor. He made no appointment to see Ford. William Knudsen was staying right where he was. This was getting to be fun now.

The price range of the new Chevrolet was $525 to $725 which compared nicely with the $495-$715 range of the year previous and permitted Chevrolet the promotional advantage of advertising a six for the price of a four. This had been the aim all along: maximum results per dollar. Although it was William Knudsen who would be described by *Fortune* magazine as "the very model for Nietzche's concept of the superman," the assignment given Chevrolet's engineering department had clearly stretched the limits of mere mortal. Getting a six for the price of a four was a phrase that slipped blithely off the tongue, getting it in reality took some doing.

With the Pontiac six experience behind them, the Chevy engineers had got down to work. There were a dozen and a half of them, and three less than a dozen prototype engines built prior to February of 1927. All of them were L-heads. That month Ormond Hunt became more involved unofficially in engineering at the corporate level, and James M. Crawford was brought in to take charge of the Chevy project. More prototypes followed. They were all L-heads too.

Jim Crawford had been an artist before becoming an engineer, and would become an artist again after retiring from General Motors in 1951. His career change had come in Indianapolis in 1909 when, after renting a studio, setting up an easel, filling empty coffee cans with oil paints and brushes, and having calling cards printed up announcing his availability for magazine illustration, he was stopped one day on the street by an acquaintance who worked for the American Motor Car Company. "You're nuts to go into that business when there's so much more to be made in automobiles," the acquaintance said, and offered him a good salary—whereon Crawford tore up his business cards, cancelled the lease on his studio, traded his easel for a drafting board and began working up ideas for the American Underslung. In 1913 he moved over to Chalmers, hopped around some after that, and then early in the Twenties went to Auburn. Errett Lobban Cord arrived soon thereafter, and the two men got on well. But, when Chevrolet beckoned, Crawford moved on again. He was convinced Chevy would beat Ford, and in fact bet Cord a silk hat that it would happen. "He never paid

51

off," Crawford would remember, although upon being reminded Cord would invariably tell him just to buy a hat and send him the bill. Crawford never did and years later, when the two men last met, Crawford again mentioned that "I never got my hat" and Cord replied that it was out of fashion by now anyway.

In 1927, however, when Chevrolet passed Ford in sales, both men had other things on their mind. Cord was sending his Auburns to race tracks throughout the East to do battle with the Stutz, and Crawford had his own battles in Michigan at Chevrolet. Early on he recognized that he could count on help from Ormond Hunt, and hindrance from Richard Grant. As overall supervisor, Hunt remained enthusiastic toward the Chevy project, and so did Grant as Chevrolet's sales major domo, but Grant did not think as an engineer. To Crawford and Hunt, an L-head six seemed the obvious way to go to meet the maximum-results-per dollar dictum. But "valves in head, ahead in value" had been Chevrolet's traditional slogan, and though Grant recognized that it was by now becoming hackneyed, he could much more easily come up with a new variation on it than a rationale for going L-head. The new Chevy six had to have overhead valves. Grant won that one.

Other means now had to be found to come up with an economical engine, and Crawford who had practiced artistic license before found himself doing it again until solutions that combined the creative and the cheap could be proved workable. A couple of these resulted in slogans that were not coined in the sales department. The material used for the pistons would give rise to "Cast Iron Wonder," and the use of ¼"-20 slotted head bolts to "Stove Bolt Six." Neither of these nicknames found much favor with Chevy people at the time. In addition to the six for the price of the four theme, Dick Grant preferred the "Outstanding Chevrolet of Chevrolet History," but neither of these had more than passing cachet. William Knudsen hated the nicknames. He'd always found "Tin Lizzie" amusing for Henry Ford's Model T. He was no longer amused.

There had been little amusement in Chevy's engineering department as the final specifications for the production six were set down. This was serious business, and the time for experimentation had drawn to a close. The production Chevy six, interestingly, shared its 3-5/16-inch bore with both the new Pontiac six and Buick's overhead valve unit; its stroke was 3¾ inches for a displacement of 194 cubic inches. Horsepower developed was 46 at 2400 rpm. Cost cutting had been seen to by such measures as the one-piece sheet metal cover for the pushrod side of the block and the cylinder head, and splash lubrication to rod bearings, with gravity feed to the three main and cam bearings. The 46-pound crankshaft was statically and dynamically balanced and forged in one plane, "a new development in the manufacture of six-cylinder crankshafts," the press said. There were weaknesses in the unit, to be sure, bottom end design probably the most serious. But overall it really was a "Cast Iron Wonder."

More important, it eliminated—as *MoToR* pointedly noted—"the biggest 'alibi feature' heretofore inseparable from the low-priced field." It replaced the four-cylinder engine and "its inevitable vibration" with the smoothness of a six. It was, *Automobile Topics* said, "an epochal achievement"—and, in retrospect, that seems not to be overstatement. If Ford gave America its first reliable cheap car, Chevrolet gave America its first civilized one. Cavilling might be in order on the adjectival terms, but historically, in the context of the respective eras the Tin Lizzie and the Cast Iron Wonder were introduced, the significance of the achievements are at the very least comparable. Certainly at the time what

1928 National Series AB Coach / Owner: Edward Basl

Chevrolet had accomplished was lost on neither the press nor the public.

In July of 1928 Walter Chrysler, as *Time* put it, had "gone into the low-priced field with the throttle wide open," but the new Plymouth wouldn't even have "floating power" until 1931, nor six cylinders until 1933. For the banner year of '29, William Knudsen didn't give a second thought to Chrysler. He really hadn't the time. He remained consumed with his first thoughts about Ford. With the new Chevy six, he was leaving the low-priced "alibi" to Dearborn. This delighted him.

And he had hedged all of his bets. He had seen the sprightly Ford Model A, he was determined the new Chevy six would be sprightlier. It was back to Harley

1929 International Series AC Four-Door Sedan / Owner: Charles Whitworth

1929 International Series AC Sport Coupe / Owner: Lew Clark

1930 Universal Series AD Coach / Owner: Gary Fling

Earl. Earl meantime had been taken along by Alfred Sloan on a whirlwind trip to Europe, and in France he talked to two coachbuilders who spoke his language, figuratively and literally. Those Americans in Paris, Tom Hibbard and Howard "Dutch" Darrin, were given an assignment for several one-offs on GM cars, including a Chevrolet sedan which was shipped to the States sometime during '28. Dutch Darrin remembers receiving a handsome retainer for all this, and finds "traces" of Hibbard & Darrin influence in the '29 Chevrolet. There were also, courtesy of Harley Earl, traces of the LaSalle which in turn of course had sported traces of Hispano-Suiza. And all of this rendered appropriate—although coincidental—the renaming of the Chevrolet line from the National Series of '28 to the International of '29.

"Richly colored, pleasingly upholstered and nicely finished both inside and out" were not terms heretofore tossed about in the press for low-priced cars, but such was the consensus about the new Chevrolet. "Emphatic improvements in dress" was the quaint way one journalist phrased it. The disc wheels on all save the sport models were *au courant*, as was the smart treatment of window reveals and swept mouldings. That the car was rich, pleasing and nice in performance too was equally lauded. Its above-60-mph maximum was a speed it could travel comfortably all day. The cars used for a special press preview at the GM Milford proving ground were test vehicles which had already been run 50,000 to 100,000 miles. One reporter noted with awe the "accelerating pump which is attached to the throttle in such a way that a quick depression of the accelerator pedal shoots a priming charger of gasoline directly into the intake manifold [and] extraordinarily rapid acceleration is produced." The Chevrolet was, William Knudsen was sure, a considerably better car than the Model A Ford.

But Knudsen was aware too that he was not the folk hero that Henry Ford was—and that he could not imprint that intangible called personality onto his car, nor expect the tangible results that this often brought. Thus he was not disappointed when the unprecedented millions who had flocked to see the new Model A did not do likewise for his car, though he did congratulate Richard Grant when, among the visitors at the Waldorf in New York, one turned out to be Vice President Charles G. Dawes. It was said that Grant had tried for President Hoover himself for the Washington, D.C. showing at the Mayflower—but Mr. Hoover alas couldn't make it.

The numbers Chevrolet promoted in the months ahead were not showroom visitors but showroom orders—and production figures. And both were impressive. In the first forty-five days the new Chevrolet six was on the assembly line, 106,914 units were produced. And there were orders on hand for many more than that.

Nonetheless, Ford with his Model A would win the sales race of '29. Once he got his production machinery in order, he could at last accommodate the hordes who had been waiting for a Ford since the T assembly line had been shut down nearly two years before. Calendar year production of the Model A for 1929 would be a tad over 1.5 million units. Chevy either missed the million mark or just made it, depending upon how the figures were juggled. Needless to say, Knudsen juggled on the high side.

Henry Ford was confident that the price differential—an approximate $100 edge depending upon body style—would keep him in the lead, and indeed it would—for 1930. William Knudsen was confident his Chevrolet would ultimately prevail, and indeed it would—in 1931.

1930 Universal Series AD Landau Sedan / Owner: Dr. J.E. Carrey

1930 Universal Series AD Roadster / Owner: William E. Taggart

1931 Independence Series AE Five-Passenger Coupe / Owner: E. Louis Munday

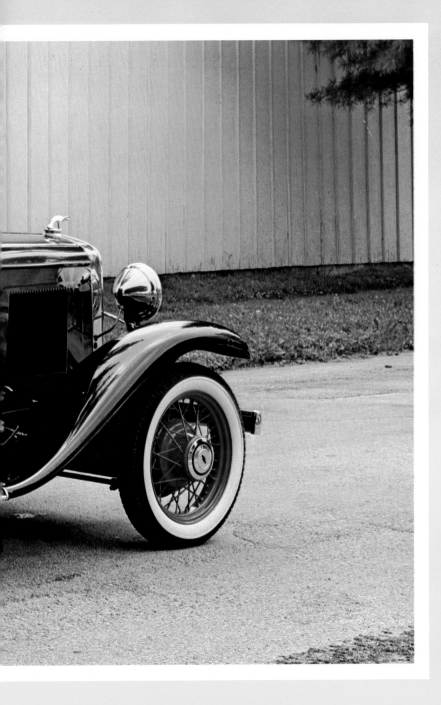

As ardently as Ford was committed to the lowest-priced car in the low-price field, Knudsen was devoted to giving the customer more for the price than he might have expected. It was a psychological ploy of sorts, illustrated well by the M.P.G. Episode. When the engineering department found to its delight that the Chevy six was providing twenty-one miles to the gallon, word was passed to the advertising department with the suggestion that the world be told, to which the admen readily agreed. "Let's say twenty," Knudsen decreed. The engineering department didn't like the idea of not getting full credit for its due, nor was the advertising department happy about not taking full advantage of a promotable statistic. But Knudsen was adamant. "I will tell you," he said. "We are making 3000 cars a day. There might be a little variation in the carburetor or the jets. If you say twenty and the customer gets twenty-one, he will probably say he is getting twenty-three. If you say twenty-one and he is getting twenty, he will swear he is getting seventeen." There's a gorgeous logic to that.

Unfortunately there wasn't a great deal of logic to much of what was happening outside of Chevrolet during 1929. But inside, matters were following a pragmatic course. The wild Chevy success of the late Twenties meant that many of its key people would be called to upper-echelon corporate duty, and in late May the official announcement came that both Ormond Hunt and Richard Grant were moving up to corporate vice-presidencies, with Jim Crawford and Harry Klingler taking over their old posts at Chevrolet. And William Knudsen appointed a long-time GM friend, Marvin E. Coyle, as Chevrolet's general auditor and vice-president.

Coyle had begun his career with a Kentucky cooperage firm carrying the delicious name of Hiram Blow & Company—and arrived in Detroit from its Terre Haute branch on Christmas Day 1911 to answer a blind ad he had seen for the accounting department of "an automobile company." Only on the day following when he drove to the appointed address did he discover that the job was at General Motors. This was, of course, in the wake of Billy Durant's initial ouster from the corporation after having wreaked financial havoc upon it, and perhaps it was thought that if a prospect wasn't told the mess he would be getting himself into he might be more likely to apply to get into it. Coyle did, got the job and rose rapidly. He was transferred to Chevrolet in 1917, soon after Billy Durant was back, and survived when Durant was booted out again. His almost total recall of production and financial statistics was the wonder of his associates. Newsmen nicknamed him "Mr. Facts and Figures." He was a terrific beancounter. But there would be fewer beans to count now. The stock market crashed in October.

"Every message radiates a complete confidence over the year's prospect," Chevrolet's new vice-president for sales remarked in January regarding what he'd been hearing from his dealers. Harry Klingler was like that. Marvin Coyle might look at his facts and figures and worry—but not Klingler. On a sales trip East that month, he stopped by the White House and afterward it was reported that he "discussed business conditions with the President." Doubtless Harry Klingler cheered Herbert Hoover up.

Harry Klingler could sell anybody or anything—rather like Billy Durant in that regard, but Klingler was not an adventurer, never sold more than he had or could handle, be it Delco lights or Murphy chairs, both of which he hustled before taking on Chevrolet. He was big and rangy and affable, with an instinctive feel for what made a good news story and a deft facility for leaking it ef-

1931 Independence Series AE Road

ner: Gordon Langeneger

1931 Independence Series AE DeLuxe Phaeton / Owner: Jim Wesbrooks

1931 Independence Series AE Sport Coupe / Owner: Earl Frey

fectively. He was equally adept at pointing out blue patches in gloomy, grey skies—and the fact that during this period William Knudsen continued his spirited playing of Souza marches on the xylophone at home every night, one sure sign always of his sanguinity, was perhaps due to Klingler's telling him everything would be all right. Probably Knudsen in any case wouldn't have allowed anything happening on Wall Street to interfere with the pleasure of his pursuit of Henry Ford.

It hadn't been necessary to change the Chevrolet much for 1930. What had been the National in '28 and the International in '29 now became the Universal Series which didn't leave much room for further variation on that theme. Variations in the car itself included revisions to the brakes (now enclosed at the rear, cable operated at the front), a heavier rear axle, larger section tires, Lovejoy hydraulic shock absorbers as standard equipment—and, in the engine, larger intake and smaller exhaust valves and manifold improvements for an increase in brake horsepower to 50 at 2600 rpm. The wheelbase remained at 107 inches.

There was a jaunty rake given the previous vertical windshield, and the gas gauge moved from the tank to the instrument panel. Mid-year, either wire or disc wheels would be optional at no extra cost. But that was about it.

More significantly, William Knudsen lowered prices—to the $495-$675 range—which brought the Chevrolet Coach within $65 of the price tag of the Ford Tudor. Only sixty-five dollars more for two more cylinders, ten more horsepower and three-and-a-half more inches of passenger room between the axles.

The seven millionth Chevrolet in its history rolled off the assembly line on May 28th, 1930—and the two millionth Chevy six on August 7th. The world's lowest priced six-cylinder automobile was doing very well. But not as well as the Model A, comparatively. There would be more than a million of the latter produced in 1930, and not quite 700,000 of the Chevrolet.

Knudsen was convinced that the Ford lead for this the second consecutive year remained as testament only to the initial delays in getting the Model A into

1931 Independence Series AE Special Sedan / Owner: Glenn Honeyman

1932 Confederate Series BA Convertible Cabriolet / Owners: Doc and Lois Hattenhauer

production; Ford was, in other words, still catching up. Still, Knudsen decided to redouble his advertising efforts—including sponsorship of a radio series called "Chevrolet Chronicles" which presented the personally narrated experiences of prominent American war veterans and was hosted by Captain Eddie Ricken- backer who had been at liberty since the demise of the car bearing his name. And, further, he decided to advance the introduction of his new Chevrolet line for '31 a full seven weeks—to November 15th. That done, he went home that night to play a particularly rousing rendition of "The Stars and Stripes Forever" on his xylophone—leaving everyone else back at Chevrolet to figure out how to get seven weeks' work done in a little less than two. Somehow they made it. Ad- vancing the date had been a great idea. The new Chevrolet for 1931 made more news that it would have otherwise.

Not that this was undeserved. Called the Independence Series now, and divided into standard and deluxe lines, the '31 Chevrolet remains in the opinion of many among the finest motorcars the marque has ever produced. With a two- inch increase in wheelbase—to 109—the cars were significantly more roomy, and their styling was clearly more dashing. Frames were stiffer, engines smoother, radiators larger, steering easier, the clutch more durable, the transmission quieter. There was more chrome, and tastefully used, including headlamp tie bar and the headlamps themselves. There was more room in the rear deck of those models with a rumble seat—Chevrolet had introduced its first rumble seat in the Sport Roadster the year previous—and more cars now available with one, including a Sport Coupe, and the Convertible Coupe in the deluxe line. A Landau Phaeton was another dashing new body style.

Among the reasons officially offered by William Knudsen for advancing the release date for the new Chevrolet was that the "extraordinary activity [it generated] for the more than 200,000 people throughout the United States who depend upon this company for their livelihood would be a distinct contribution to the cause of general business." He of course mentioned nothing about Henry Ford and the sales race—but assuredly he had an Olympics-calibre runner this time, and he wanted to get it out there.

The new Chevrolet was even less expensive too, prices ranging from a high of $650 to a low of $475. No Chevrolet in history had ever sold for as little. And the previous lowest-priced Chevrolet—the Four-Ninety introduced in 1915—had seldom even carried that price tag. William Knudsen thought he could sell a million of these new cars.

Harry Klingler had told him so. But even Harry Klingler was less ebullient than usual now. "The business depression of the past year is being prolonged by persons of prominence and authority thinking and talking depression," he remarked to his dealers at the new-car preview during the month of November. "By virtue of their positions, they have attracted a sufficient public following to delay the inevitable upturn." But Harry was Harry, and the upturn was, of course, under way.

In January it seemed to be. William Knudsen announced with pride that "we have now taken back all of our regular employees on whole or part-time work and further increases in production will be made by increasing the number of hours of work by those departments still working part-time." At the annual show-week dealer dinner, the talk of business conditions was brief, most of the evening's program given over to entertainment, including the presentation of Frank Finn, a twelve-year-old vocalist, the "protégé of the New Haven zone."

By May Chevrolet was operating on a full-time basis, in early June in the belief that "the potential buying capacity of the Country is unimpaired," Harry Klingler announced an extensive program for his 35,000 dealers ("Chevrolet To Take Million for a Ride" was his press release headline), and later that month poured more money into advertising, noting that the American Tobacco Com- pany and the National Biscuit Company had also effectively boosted their ad- vertising expenditures. "There is ample evidence to prove," he said, "that the way out of the depression is by backing a worthy product by intensive and in- telligent merchandising."

When the figures were totted up at the end of 1931, they didn't reach the million units which had been Knudsen's and Klingler's hope. But at 627,104, they were less than 50,000 off the 1930 total. Ford production had been halved, to 541,615. Chevrolet had first place again. Although he hadn't noted it the first time around, in thanking his dealers for their efforts, William Knudsen ac- knowledged that Chevrolet's victory in the sales race this year was the first in which "our principal competitor was in active production." In Dearborn Henry had been making all the Model A Fords he could sell.

But Henry Ford wasn't thinking much about his Model A anymore. He was thinking if it was cylinders the people wanted, it was cylinders they would get. At Highland Park, Walter Chrysler was thinking the same thing—only two less. Since few things remain a secret long in the automobile industry, news of all this had reached Chevrolet.

Originally few changes had been planned for the '32 line, other than a series designation revision from Independence to Confederate. But with the rumors of cylinder proliferation among its competitors, Chevrolet got to work fast. And got its new and improved product out early. Twenty-five thousand teaser posters—a total length of 118 miles of them, as computed by Klingler—were plastered in towns of 15,000 population and over on November 28th. "Keep Your Eye on Chevrolet" was the message—and it was repeated the following evening in spot announcements over 168 radio stations. A few days later there were full-page ads in 5355 daily and weekly newspapers across the country. The results were overwhelming.

"Chevrolets for 1932 incorporate a really astonishing number of refinements, some of them totally unexpected in a car of its class and wholly surprising, from the standpoint of value received," said *Automobile Topics*. The St. Louis *Post- Dispatch* headlined, "Chevrolet Six Lacks Hardly Any Feature Found on Costly Cars."

Downdraft carburetion and manifolding, increased valve lift and a higher compression ratio contributed to 60 bhp at 3000 rpm—and an easy 70 mph, and 0-35 acceleration in 6.7 seconds. Crankcase and blocks were strengthened by ex- ternal ribs and an increase in metal thickness, there were now thin-wall main bearings, the crankshaft was counterweighted, and the engine was mounted on rubber at four points, replacing the former three-point solid system. Main and camshaft bearings were now pressure lubricated. Synchromesh transmission was combined with a free-wheeling which was described as "simple in its opera- tion as the turning of a calendar in a cardboard tube." The frame was heftier, there were larger tires on smaller wheels, cowl ventilators, door-type hood louvers, inside sun visors, a bolder rake to the windshield, a built-in radiator screen grille, and a fresh and stylish overall look which bore more than a familial resemblance to the cars General Motors was selling in its higher class markets.

1932 Confederate Series BA Coach / Owner: Howard Pyle

1932 Confederate Series BA Coupe / Owner: Ken Colpean

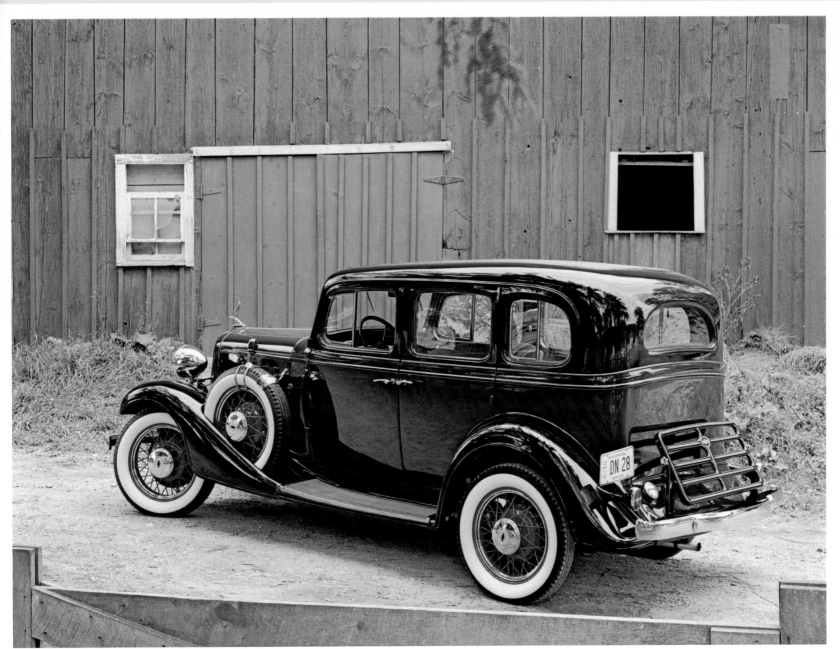

1933 Master Series CA Sedan / Owner: Grady Burch

1933 Master Series CA Sport Roadster / Owner: Wayne McKinley

For two months Chevrolet basked in the laurels of its marvelous new line. Then in mid-February Henry Ford let it be known that he had a new V-8 upon which he was willing to "risk all" for the good of America because "you know, faith is catching." Thereafter, the press gushed forth tales of the "American Moses leading his people out of the Land of Depressed Bondage"—while everyone everywhere waited for the V-8 to appear, and everyone at Chevrolet gnashed their teeth. Henry Ford sure knew how to make headlines.

Meanwhile, some counter measures were tried. Prices were dropped fifty dollars or so, which was a case of "Chevrolet Making Hay," as *Automobile Topics* put it, without adding the usual figurative qualifier. The qualifier came the last day of March when the sun shone and more than five and a half million people rushed out to see the new Ford V-8. It had five more horsepower than the Chevy six, but it was three inches shorter in wheelbase. It did not have the hydraulic brakes the Plymouth had since its inception, but the Plymouth was still a four. Both Chevrolet and Ford had doubtless been relieved to learn that Plymouth's new six was a model year away.

Not that much of any of this made a difference in 1932. Although William Knudsen might "be pleased to be able to report that no Chevrolet employees have been thrown on their communities for charity," the situation in America was desperate. Harry Klingler was distraught. America would enjoy normal conditions again, he said, only when the automobile industry was brought back to normalcy—a logic that another GM man would later echo more quotably regarding "what's good for General Motors."

There were the occasional glimmers of optimism. Swift & Company bought a thousand new Chevy cars and trucks—the division's commercial line had been considerably revamped and reduced in price as well for '32—and because fleet sales had been among the first to plummet in the wake of the stock market crash, Harry Klingler took this as a sign that things might be getting better. That they were instead getting worse had been more formidably signalled in late spring when Alfred Sloan announced the General Motors plan which consolidated Buick, Oldsmobile and Pontiac sales under the hated and short-lived B.O.P. administration, and coordinated Chevrolet and Oakland (Pontiac) manufacturing operations under the direction of William Knudsen.

Knudsen scarcely needed the extra work. There wasn't much business to be had anywhere, and what there was required herculean efforts to get. Chevrolet got it. In mid-'32 it was selling one out of every three cars produced in America, and by year's end that ratio had not changed significantly. But the overall figures for '32 were devastating—300,000-odd Chevrolets, 200,000-odd Fords, 100,000-odd Plymouths. Everyone else in the industry was building only in the tens of thousands, if that. Chevrolet still had first place, but it really didn't seem to matter. The country was in shambles. There was a new President about to enter the White House who was determined to change things and who thought fear itself was the nation's only real trepidation.

The people at Chevrolet had to fear Henry Ford. No one ever could be sure what he would do next. His unpredictability was awesome. The Ford V-8 had had a difficult borning year, there were the usual production delays—and in February of 1933 there was the by-now-usual delayed presentation of the Ford for the new model year. Its wheelbase was increased to 112 inches and it now had 75 hp. Walter Chrysler's new Plymouth six was already out; it had 70 hp and a 107-inch wheelbase and, when it didn't catch on, the car was stretched into a 112-

inch Deluxe model offered in a bewildering array of exterior color and interior upholstery combinations which, once customers deciphered how to order them and the factory how to make them up, resulted in a low-priced car that was a virtual custom job. *MoToR* saw the coming year as a "Three-Ring Battle."

Chevrolet's entry, which had preceded the others into the marketplace, indicated that the grapevine perhaps had not been as reliable as heretofore. The new Chevrolet had a 65 hp engine and a 110-inch wheelbase. The added power had been seen to by lengthening the stroke to four inches, for 206.8 cubic inches; the compression ratio remained at 5.2 to one, the rated power was now delivered at 3000 rpm. The extra inch added to the wheelbase was sufficient to allow for longer, lower and wider Fisher bodies, which were fitted with the new "no-draft" ventilation. The new styling was, *Automobile Topics* said, "a Chevrolet à la mode, for it has the Van Dyke front, the flowing lines, skirted wheel shrouds and neatly tailored back that is strictly of the moment." The new accelerator-operated starter was called, logically enough, the "Starterator"—and "Stanamic" balance was the name given the new engine mounts, "coined from the static and dynamic engine forces which the mounting is designed to isolate." Prices were raised, then lowered, then raised again, then lowered. It was the same throughout the industry.

Of one thing, Chevrolet was certain. The division wanted a vehicle that it could price more competitively from the beginning, and "a new small car to be known as the Mercury model" was rumored in February. It arrived in March, as the Standard Six, which elevated the larger six to Master. ("Eagle" and "Mercury" ostensibly took over from "Confederate" as the series' names but they would not be widely used.) The Standard's price range was $445-$475, fifty dollars less than the Master, which bought a car with a 107-inch wheelbase and 60 hp engine (a shorter 3½-inch stroke, 180.86 cubic inches, smaller crankshaft bearings, but otherwise numerous interchangeable parts). It had neither free wheeling, nor synchromesh transmission, nor "Starterator"—it used hood louvers instead of doors, headlamps were painted black and the horn was put under the hood. It was a car, Chevrolet said, "pointed primarily at the fleet market, the commercial traveler and the buyer desiring a personal car of low first cost." But the real point was to come up with anything that might spur sales.

The Standard helped, and though the bank moratorium hindered the clearing of cars to dealers initially, it did seem that the corner to better times was at least being approached. In the meantime, Chevrolet began installing equipment in Chicago for the assembly line which would be among the more fascinating exhibits of the Century of Progress world's fair, and in Washington, industry executives were hammering out the automobile code of the National Industrial Recovery Act.

Nineteen thirty-three ended rather as 1932 had—Chevrolet, followed by Ford and Plymouth. The figures were a little better though, 481,134, 339,969 and 255,564. Plymouth had come on strong (better than double the year previous), Ford had improved some. But Chevy remained first. Keeping it there, however, would now be someone else's job.

In October William Knudsen was appointed executive vice-president of General Motors Corporation. And William Knudsen almost immediately decided the person who could best take charge of the troubled Pontiac division was Harry Klingler.

A new captain and a new cheerleader would have to be found for Chevrolet. 69

CHAPTER FOUR

CHEVROLET

GETTING THE FIX ON FIRST

Chevrolet Rides Through the Thirties

Marvin Coyle celebrated his forty-sixth birthday on October 8th, 1933. Exactly one week later he was named the new general manager of Chevrolet. He was a *rara avis* for such a position in General Motors. For one thing, he was comparatively young. For another, he was an accountant. Those characteristics combined in one man had never made it to the top of any GM division before. But Chevrolet couldn't have chosen any man better for William Knudsen's old job.

Immediately after the Coyle announcement, William E. Holler was selected to fill Harry Klingler's post as general sales manager. Formerly Chevrolet's assistant general sales manager for the eastern half of the United States, Holler had been waving the Chevrolet banner since 1925, and in the eight years following had frequently handled troubleshooting assignments that would have stymied a lesser man. Chevrolet couldn't have chosen more wisely in this instance either.

Marvin Coyle was the sort who would gently pat his Chevrolet (he drove nothing else) and murmur, "It's a good product." William Holler was the sort who would slap its fender and bellow, "Chevrolet is the best damn car on the market today!"

Chevrolet had its new captain and its new cheerleader.

Although he was little known outside the industry, Marvin Coyle was well respected within it. Since 1929 he had been, quite literally, William Knudsen's understudy, and when Chevrolet's star was away Coyle performed his role. In fact, for nearly six months the year past, when Knudsen lay seriously ill with kidney stones, what Coyle had been was de facto head of Chevrolet. Though his accent was strictly Indiana, and he was not given to dramatics of any kind, probably the most self-effacing executive in the GM hierarchy, and although he had no aptitude for the xylophone, Marvin Coyle and William Knudsen were very much alike in other respects. Highly literate and self-educated men, they shared an affection for the works of Voltaire, Aristotle, Kipling, Chesterton, Bacon and Twain. They had been devoted friends for so long, and had worked so closely together at Chevrolet, that most people wouldn't recognize even the transition from the one man's leaving to the other's taking over.

Marvin Coyle had learned accounting the same way he had learned French and English history, and the mechanical arts—the further subjects he enjoyed. He taught himself. Thus, although he was kidded as "Mr. Facts and Figures" and decimal points not corpuscles were said to run in his blood, he knew more about the beans he was counting than just how to count them. He had the feel for what Chevrolet was—and the sense of organization and priority that would keep the machinery running smoothly. When the onslaught of the Great Depression meant that cost-cutting measures were necessary to lower the break-even point to the 400,000-unit range, he saw that it was done without perceptible diminution of the product. Like Knudsen, he was a big man, sturdily built, but less prepossessing—the Dean Jagger-fatherly sort. He had the wit of an Irishman, a calm self-assurance, and a straight-from-the-shoulder forthrightness. "There is no such thing as brilliance in this business," he said. "It's purely a matter of luck and avoiding blunders." Doubtless no criticism of Henry Ford was intended—unlike Knudsen, Coyle probably never lost any sleep wondering what Ford might do next. His only concern was his own next move. In his first interview with newsmen after taking charge at Chevrolet, he said frankly, "There is only one way the new car price can go with increased costs of operations under the automobile code." And he pointed his finger skyward. Newsmen were not accustomed to such candor. Several of them suggested Coyle was rather like the Chevrolet. No nonsense.

So was Chevrolet's new general sales manager, the aptly named William Holler. Like Harry Klingler, enthusiastic overstatement was his forte, and he practiced it frequently in no fewer than three speeches in three different places a day. He was a thriving workaholic—and his rah-rah and slap-on-the-back approach was bolstered by a solid comprehension of what an aggressive sales network should be. He did well by his dealers—and he was immensely popular with them.

William E. Holler   *Marvin E. Coyle*

At the annual preview for dealers in early December 1933, Bill Holler had promised his sales force that the Chevrolet would be "basically, radically and decidedly different for 1934." Actually, this wasn't so much overstatement as a spirited telling of the way it was—and one of the Chevrolet's most salient and saleable new features had been a parting present to the division by William Knudsen.

In March of 1933, after witnessing a demonstration, Knudsen fell in love with independent front suspension. So did the general managers of the other GM divisions, who did not think the corporation's bread-and-butter car should have it too. There was considerable argument on the subject. Maurice Olley, who had developed i.f.s. for GM, was in on the contretemps. As the other general managers argued top-of-the-line exclusivity, and even old Chevy man Ormond Hunt questioned whether there were enough machines in the United States to

take care of grinding the wire of coil springs on Chevy's mass basis, Knudsen stood firm. The machine tool industry had been in a bad way for years, he countered, Chevy going i.f.s. would help them out. And the argument raged on. As Maurice Olley remembered, "Bill Knudsen declared in words of one syllable that Chevrolet was not going to be left out!"

Chevy's chief engineer Jim Crawford was all for the idea too. "The bigger you are, the fewer chances you take," he had said often—but Knee-Action was too good to pass up. So Knudsen went into battle once more; a few more words of one syllable, vigorously said, did the trick. The system for Chevrolet was based on Dubonnet principles, using coil-sprung trailing arms and integral shock absorbers.

It was a good thing Knudsen had been so obstinate. For Plymouth sported i.f.s. for '34 as well, which left Henry Ford to grouse that "we use transverse springs for the same reason that we use round wheels—because we have found nothing better for the purpose." The Plymouth six was up to 77 hp, 82 with optional aluminum head; Ford's V-8, with dual downdraft carburetor and dual intake manifold, was up to 85 hp—and an 87 mph maximum.

Chevy had more power too. There had been a "Blue Streak" added to the Cast Iron Wonder—and it developed 80 horsepower and guaranteed 80 miles an hour. No dimensional or displacement changes were involved, just very clever combustion chamber redesign which had resulted from a "practice assignment," as Jim Crawford called it, of a few years previous to design "a race-type engine with very small piston displacement . . . which would deliver exceptionally higher power." Since this demanded larger valves, in the new head design the exhaust valves were set at an angle and close to the spark plugs, and the intakes were straight. Thus detonation was controlled by the exhaust valve starting combustion while the cool intake valve concomitantly retarded its final stages. Power was saved, economy was achieved, and volumetric efficiency was high. For some inexplicable reason, probably conjured in the advertising department, Blue Streak would become Blue Flame by 1935.

Certainly explicable for '34 was the wheelbase increase to 112 inches. It made for more room inside, a more sleek and streamlined appearance outside—and an on-a-par dimension with Ford and Plymouth. Hood louvers went horizontal and "airfoil type," and Knee-Action necessitated a modified X-frame with a new cross member, which made it a YK.

Although no names would be thought up for Chevrolets this year (the Master was just that and no more), when the Standard was introduced, special mention was made of the revival of a "historic figure . . . which was the magic that brought [Chevrolet] fame now almost twenty years ago." It was 490, and it was the price of the least expensive Standard model (the sport roadster)—and perhaps this historical aside (maybe even the price) was tossed out to mitigate the effect of the Chevrolet prices having been raised this year, about forty dollars, as Marvin Coyle had said they inexorably would. The Standard coupe was $510, the coach and phaeton $520. Master Series Chevrolets were from $85 to $95 more.

Prices were raised generally throughout the industry that spring, then in early summer they were reduced back to where they had been at the first of the year. **71**

1934 Master Series DA Four-Door Sedan / Owner: Jim Mix

1935 Standard Series EC Phaeton / Owners: Mr. and Mrs. Homer H. Leiser

1936 Standard Series FC Town Sedan / Owner: Roy Strevel, Jr.

In the press the Chevrolet cuts were "interpreted generally as an answer to increasingly successful Ford competition." The interpretation was probably correct. Marvin Coyle continued to regard the break-even point carefully; though the economy seemed to be lifting, there remained considerable uncertainty. He wanted his cars priced just right—low enough to be stalwart competitors, high enough to cushion any sudden sales downturn. His new cuts put a few of his Standards below similar models in the Ford line, a few of them above. A happy medium, he thought.

The V-8 Ford by now had begun to make a competition name for itself, and a phenomenal one. Chevrolet elected to leave that field to Ford, and attract a few headlines itself by taking what had originated as "a local stunt feature last year by a photographer of a Dayton paper" and turning it into the All-American Soap Box Derby. Thousands of entries poured into Chevrolet offices, and even Chevy engineers were impressed, so much so with the efforts of twelve-year-old Jack Nicholas of Indianapolis who, with the aid of his father, had constructed his racer for a total cost of fifteen cents, that young Nicholas was invited to Detroit to be a luncheon guest. Marvin Coyle talked to him, and so did Jim Crawford. Conceivably they wanted to learn a few of his cost-cutting measures. The first Derby, however, was won by an eleven-year-old from Muncie, Indiana, who had lavished seven dollars on his racer.

Manufacturing economy in Chevrolet's chosen field was the paramount consideration. And it was a limitation on Jim Crawford's design freedom which he apparently accepted with equanimity. His reputation was as a hard-nosed engineer. "We don't want a sissy," said Marvin Coyle. The two men got along well. Since that day, years before, when Crawford lost the argument to sales manager Dick Grant about whether the new Chevy six should be L-head or overhead-valve, Crawford had lost few others. Disgruntled murmurs from sales people that the way to handle Ford's V-8 was with two more cylinders of their own were summarily dismissed—likewise were suggestions that the Plymouth provided its advertising department with more engineering niceties to talk about. Crawford was not flashy. Neither was the Chevrolet.

Indeed precisely why the Chevrolet was so popular was somewhat of a puzzle. The V-8 sold because it was a Ford, it had the imprint of Henry Ford's personality, in a way his temperament too, and it was the hottest low-priced car in America. The Plymouth sold because it was an upstart bursting with innovations, the product of one of the industry's boy wonders who had not yet grown up sufficiently to realize that prudence suggested throwing hydraulic brakes, full pressure lubrication, aluminum alloy pistons and an independent hand brake all into one car (which Chrysler had done with his very first Plymouth in 1928) was really overkill. But why did people buy Chevrolets? Later in the decade, *Fortune* magazine would suggest that it was because "the Chevrolet car probably has fewer enemies than any car made . . . [it is] the greatest common denominator of what the American public thinks a good car ought to be."

That was as good a reason as any, one supposes, and in 1934 it was sufficient for triumph once more in the production race: Chevrolet, 620,726; Ford, 563,-921; Plymouth, 351,113. Industry production overall had improved and it appeared America was beginning to find its way out of the Great Depression. Maybe this was the opportune time to try something a little flashy.

Ironically, Chevrolet tried precisely the reverse. For 1935 it cut the "knees" out from under a Master, and reintroduced the car with a solid front axle, priced about twenty dollars less than the i.f.s. Master. Conventional semi-elliptic leaf spring suspension was retained throughout the Standard line. The reason for the "Master without knees" is difficult to fathom. The price differential was not significant, though there might have been the curious rationale that independent front suspension could have some "enemies" in the marketplace and Chevrolet wanted to provide a Master for them.

What Chevrolet would not provide for '35 was much variety for the enthusiast of open-air motoring: nothing at all in the Master line, and the Standard sport roadster and phaeton body styles would have a limited run which would end early in the model year. By default, then, Chevrolet relinquished to Ford—with its half dozen or so open cars—an entire segment of the market. Although that market was a small one, it did have cachet and did draw most of the young people of the era who were able to afford any car at all. Plymouth had not built an open car since '32, but it had an engineering panache which appealed to the more sophisticated motorist of limited means. Chevrolet in '35 seemed strictly old folks.

What Chevrolet did positively rather than negatively in '35 was well summarized by *The Automobile Trade Journal*: "Whereas last year the two Chevrolet chassis models were identical in general appearance but differed greatly in performance, this year the two cars differ radically in appearance but are fairly well on a par with each other on performance." The Standard was given the Master's engine, but with smaller intake manifold and carburetor, for 75 hp at 3200 rpm vis-à-vis the Master's 80 at 3300. The Master was given the new Fisher "Turret Top" and brand-new styling on a 113-inch wheelbase, including vee-windshield and "suicide" doors. The Standard for '35 looked like the Standard for '34. The Master's engine of '35 was merely refined over the '34, a new pressure jet system of lubrication for connecting rods being a decided improvement.

There was nothing untoward about the Chevrolets for 1935, nothing unexpected, and this was perhaps the reason that Ford won the sales race. The new Model 48 V-8 had 90 hp, and a new wrinkle called "Center-Poise" which friendly critics said was tantamount to independent springing of all four wheels, though not very convincingly. Still, the Ford V-8 had pizzazz—and in a year when improvement in the economy made that an appealing commodity, Dearborn prevailed. The year-end figures were Ford, 942,439; Chevrolet, 793,437; Plymouth, 442,281.

That this had been anticipated early in the year at Chevrolet was apparent. Even Bill Holler wasn't his usual boisterous self at dealer gatherings held after the debut of the new Ford, and his standing ovations which were the usual were unusually subdued. Certainly the labor situation, which affected Chevrolet particularly, was nettlesome and upset orderly production plans, but by mid-May the last of the Chevrolet holdouts returned to work when the AFL union at Cincinnati voted unanimously to call off the strike there. That the principal problem was the Chevrolet and not the producing of it had seemed obvious the month previous when, at the dedication of a new Chevrolet assembly plant in Baltimore, GM president Sloan himself felt called upon to inform dealers that next year's Chevrolets "will be all that you hope they will be." Since this was April, and the cars were not scheduled for introduction until November, the press puzzled over this "first public reference which any manufacturer has made to the . . . 1936 models." Sloan offered no details for obvious reasons, among

1936 Standard Series FC Convertible Cabriolet / Owner: Robert Nadler

1936 One-Half Ton Pickup in t

1937 Master DeLuxe Series

Door Sedan / Owner: W.H. Heinrich

1937 Master Series GB Coach / Owner: Merrill Jones

them that he didn't know what the '36 cars would be. Neither did anyone at Chevrolet precisely at that point.

Marvin Coyle didn't panic. He got his facts and figures together, began studying them—and told Bill Holler to do the best he could with what he had. Advertising and promotion expenditures were increased—and in July Holler went to Washington, D.C. to talk J. Edgar Hoover into opening his files for him so that Chevrolet could sponsor what Holler knew would be a smash radio series: "G-Men . . . actual cases from the official files of the Federal Bureau of Investigation." In this the era of Bonnie and Clyde, and Dillinger, the FBI was as saleable as the Chevrolet. The association between them wouldn't hurt. It was widely known that the "bad guys" drove Ford V-8's; Clyde Barrow had even written Henry Ford a nice letter saying that he did. In June the Ford Motor Company announced that it had perfected a new rust-proofing process. Bill Holler made a few phone calls, and in September announced that Chevrolet had a new rust-proofing process too.

What the Chevrolet for 1936 had that the Ford did not was a hydraulic brake system. Probably had not Henry Ford been even more recalcitrant regarding hydraulics (the V-8 wouldn't have them until 1939), Chevrolet would not have had anything truly promotable for '36. As it was, the '36 Chevy could be advertised as "the Safest car that money can buy!"—because "Its New Perfected Hydraulic Brakes—exclusive to Chevrolet in its price range—give unequalled stopping power." This was a convenient forgetting of the Plymouth which had had hydraulics all along, though perhaps the "New Perfected" took care of that, with a hint that Walter Chrysler had introduced his version unperfected. Surrounding passengers "with the safety of steel" in the Turret Top Body, and the Fisher No Draft Ventilation System which "protects health by giving passengers individually controlled ventilation without drafts," remained genuine low-priced exclusives. And the Knee-Action Ride at Chevrolet remained exclusive only to the Master.

Otherwise the Master and Standard series were more alike than ever this year. The latter was given the styling treatment awarded to the Master the year before, including the Turret Top—with a little facelifting all around. The engines remained the same, but with a higher compression ratio (6.0 to one) and there was full-length water jacketing (which had been a Plymouth selling point for '35) for better cooling. The only readily discernible difference between the two cars was wheelbase; the Master remained at 113, the Standard was boosted up to 109. One of the latter cars was a cabriolet, which was clearly an afterthought. It was announced "for immediate introduction" four months after the rest of the line, and was probably the result of dealer requests following previews of the new cars the previous October—at which, incidentally, Bill Holler's standing ovation was more heartfelt than the year before.

Nineteen thirty-six was strictly a remedial year for Chevrolet. The embarrassment of losing first to Ford—and it was more that than debacle, it had been a profitable year—did not send Marvin Coyle into a dither of ill-considered changes immediately. His reaction had been a measured one, and he calmly proceeded to do the rectifying necessary. Henry Ford had always said that he didn't care what his competitors did—and in a way Marvin Coyle didn't either. He just wanted to be number one.

Ford helped in '36. His V-8 was scarcely changed, there was nothing new to entice, and so what Coyle had seen done to the Chevy six was enough for first

1938 Master Series HB Business Coupe / Owner: Harold Byer

1938 Master Series HB Four-Door Sedan / Owner: George L. Gosheff

81

1938 Master DeLuxe Series HA Police Car / Owner: Indiana State Police

place again. He had avoided blunders—and he'd had a little luck. The Marvin Principle had worked beautifully. But to ensure that 1935 wouldn't happen again, there was need for more than the remedial. Jim Crawford and crew were already working on it.

Insofar as the world outside Chevrolet was aware, America's once-again number one carmaker was playing it low-keyed. With Ford having nothing much new to advertise, nor Plymouth either (people at Chevrolet remained convinced Walter Chrysler had put too many of his eggs in one basket early on), Chevy's advertising department talked up hydraulics and nostalgia, and had a very good year.

The nostalgia was effectively spaced. In March, after a months-long and well-publicized campaign to find the owner of the oldest Chevrolet in licensed use in America, Hiram H. Dohner, a seventy-year-old carpenter from the little village of Quentin in Lebanon County, Pennsylvania was found. A movie casting director couldn't have auditioned anyone better for the part. He got into his 1913 Royal Mail touring car (serial number 470) and drove to Detroit, where he was presented a new 1936 Standard sedan, for which he said thank you very much, he'd be delighted to have a second car, but he had no intention of giving up his Royal Mail.

And he explained why in a little yarn that was homespun with the help of Chevy PR and which concluded with this delectable summation: "During the past 22 years, I have been able to work at carpentering pretty steady. I have earned from $900 to $1100 per year. One year I made $1500. It was all made possible by my car. In its life it has enabled me to earn about $20,000 in wages, to live happily with my wife in Quentin where that income was sufficient for our needs and it cost us only $775 added to $250 in 22 years in return for 250,000 miles of transportation."

That's the kind of advertising for the kind of car the Chevy was that couldn't be bought with the personal delivery of an apple pie to every household in America.

The second bit of nostalgia is perhaps that only in retrospect. In June the former plant of Durant Motors in Oakland, California was bought by General Motors for Chevrolet truck assembly. The historic significance of this—that it was Billy Durant who had built Hiram Dohner's Royal Mail as well as all the Chevrolets of the marque's borning years—was noted fleetingly and carefully; there were still those in the GM hierarchy who preferred to forget that the Durant era had happened at all. The 12,000,000th car to be produced since Billy Durant founded the company was, naturally, given a grand send-off from the assembly line in August.

By October, however, at the three-day national sales convention in Detroit, nostalgia having effectively marked it thus far, the time was now to talk of what was coming. Marvin Coyle said that $26 million in tooling had been spent, Bill Holler said, "wait'll you see it!" It was the new Chevrolet for 1937, and its debut would be celebrated on November 7th with 50,000 employees the guests at several thousand "Chevrolet Breakfasts" from coast to coast.

Everything about the Chevrolet for '37 seemed new, and everything about it seemed right. There was a new engine: 3½ by 3¾ inches for 216.5 cubic inches and 85 hp at 3200 rpm, with a compression ratio of 6.25 to one. It was compact, about two inches shorter than the previous six. It had four main bearings; and, though still cast iron, the domed pistons were lighter, with cutaway slipper-type

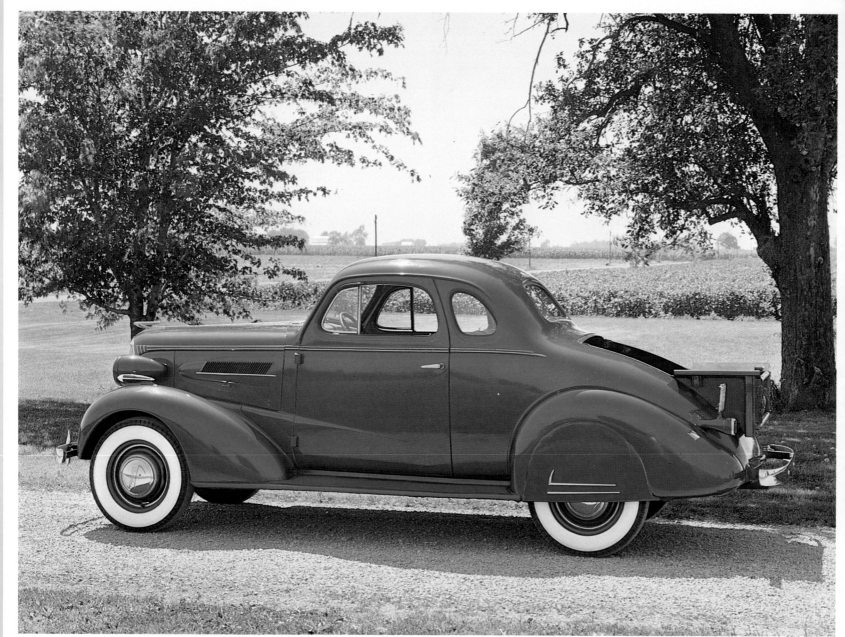

1937 Master Series GB Coupe Delivery / Owner: Robert Nadler

1939 One-Half Ton Pickup in the JC Series / Owner: Gilbert M. Laird

1939 Master 85 Series JB Business Coupe / Owner: W.H. Heinrich

1939 Master DeLuxe Series JA Sport Sedan / Owner: Merrill Jones

1940 Special DeLuxe Series KA Convertible Coupe / Owner: Mark Wilson

skirts reinforced by integral cast ribs. Connecting rods were shorter and stiffer. The counterbalanced crankshaft was equipped with a new lighterweight and more sensitive harmonic balancer. Both oil and water pumps were improved, and so was manifolding to give better thermostatic heat control. Even the air cleaner was better, with an easily removable filtering element. The Cast Iron Wonder was more wonderful yet.

A more compact and rigidly constructed synchromesh transmission was featured, the synchronizing mechanism simplified through the use of improved cone clutches. The new rear axle was of the hypoid type, previously used by such as Chrysler, Packard and Pierce-Arrow, but this year adopted by the lower-echelon Chrysler Corporation cars, Studebaker, by Chevrolet wholly and Buick and Cadillac in selected models. (Ford would not have a hypoid axle until after the war.)

The frame was all-new too. Derived from the ladder-type of the 1936 Standard, it was stiffened with box-girder siderails and four-boxed cross members. The previous YK configuration (the "Y" behind the transmission, the "K" up front) had been cumbersome and expensive, but necessary because of the Master's Dubonnet suspension. Marvin Coyle had never liked its cost, and had asked Jim Crawford to come up with something better about the time the first YK's were moving down the assembly line. Crawford ran up a ladder frame that was put on the '36 Standard, which because of its I-beam front axle worked just fine. With the advent of the all-steel body, and a little redesigning of the cross members, that basic idea now proved workable with i.f.s.—it was simpler, lighter, stronger, and less expensive to boot. Marvin Coyle was delighted.

The new hypoid axle lowered the floor some two inches, and the new frame permitted moving everything forward for more interior space, which was further enhanced by the four additional inches of overall body width (and rear-door length in the sedans) that was enjoyed by the new '37's over the previous year's model.

And there was a very admirable rationalization of the Chevrolet lines for reasons of manufacturing economy and efficiency, though how the sales department told the story was strictly Artful Dodger. There was just one Chevrolet chassis, of 112¼-inch wheelbase. The two cars put on it were identical save for trim and accessory equipment. And front suspension, which was the Artful Dodger part. The solid-axle car was now the Master—but it was not the former Master without knees, but instead the former Standard, that designation being summarily dropped. The former Master became the Master DeLuxe, and there was no Master DeLuxe without knees—the former Master without knees being simply the Master, which of course was the Standard. There were two other differences between new Master and Master DeLuxe (3.73 versus 4.22 rear axle ratio, worm and roller versus worm and sector steering) which were not nearly so confusing. The new styling was called diamond crown speedline, a pretension equal to Chevrolet's promotional insistence that the Standard no longer existed, but the styling itself was straightforward, modern and altogether pleasant.

The Chevrolet for '37 was extraordinarily well received. The top-of-the-line Master Sedan DeLuxe was tested by numerous magazines in England (the "enthusiast" press had, alas, long since ceased to exist in America), and the reviews were raves. Said *The Motor*: "This car may well set a fashion in reverting to the high top gear, which used to be available on cars of high horsepower, but which has been sacrificed in recent years to flexibility. This Chevrolet

1941 Special DeLuxe Series AH Five-Passenger Coupe / Owner: Robert E. Stremmel

pulls a 3.72 to 1 top gear which endows it with an effortlessness of cruising above 60 mph; which persuades the driver that it would be impossible to tire the car no matter how hard he drove."

The Hon. Maynard Greville, in *Country Life*, commented on the same subject: "The pleasant features of the high top-gear ratio were, first of all, the high cruising speed with low engine revolutions, and absence of engine noise and fuss; the excellent petrol consumption for so large an engine, as, on give-and-take roads, with the car being driven hard, I found I was getting well over twenty miles to the gallon; and the fact that low engine speed must always improve the wearing qualities."

The Autocar's testers were astonished to find that the Chevrolet's speedometer actually read *slow* (the italics are *The Autocar*'s). They were sorry only that the condition of the Brooklands track didn't allow them to use the car to its maximum.

Everything pointed to a million-car year and first place in sales. The latter was easily taken care of—neither Ford nor Plymouth had anything so comparably "new"—but the former fell victim to the beginnings of a business recession which had set in. The recession was taken in stride at Chevrolet. The purpose of Bill Holler's annual party for the press which, as one of its members said,

"no newspaperman willingly misses," was simply to have a good time—and Bill Holler talked as much about the fifteen-year-old from Kroonstad in the Orange Free State who had won the South African finals of the Chevrolet-sponsored Soap Box Derby, which had by now moved to Akron and become international, as he did about the cars that were being built in Detroit.

Prior to the introduction of the '38 line, Marvin Coyle seemed particularly sanguine. The reason for it was apparent in the speech given by Chevy veteran and now GM corporate vice-president of sales Richard Grant. There had been a choice the year before between spending for the Chevrolet or spending for the capacity to build it. "It was determined to first build a car that would be highly saleable," explained Grant. "By not increasing capacity, many sales were lost during the year due to the shortage of cars, but Chevrolet did attain a dominant sales position which will stand it in good stead when and as the next business slump comes." That didn't speak well for GM confidence in America, but it spoke volumes for Chevrolet.

Chevrolet was most anxious to get the new cars out. When Harley Earl and company at Art and Colour tarried, Jim Crawford just went ahead and had the radiator grille styled in the engineering department—and probably was delighted afterward when the Chevy front-end treatment was widely judged the

90

1941 Special DeLuxe Series AH Five-Passenger Coupe / Owner: Rodney Gott

1942 Fleetline Sedan in Special DeLuxe Series BH / Owner: W.H. Heinrich

most aesthetically pleasing of the car's styling features. His department also came up with a new diaphragm spring-type clutch which was cutely named "Tiptoe-matic." Both *The Autocar* and *The Motor* were as pleased with the new '38 as they had been with the '37—and would be with the '39.

Obviously Chevrolet felt on solid ground now. There was no looking back—to Ford or 1935. From we-can't-let-that-happen-again, the tenor changed to of-course-it-won't-happen-again. The switch for '39 to a conventional coil and wishbone suspension replacing the Dubonnet arrangement was forthrightly made. Though more expensive, the Dubonnet had earlier been preferred because it could be preassembled in a sealed housing, which the wishbone could not, and was thus the wiser solution since the unit would have to be shipped to eleven various assembly points in the United States. When engineers figured out how to preassemble the cross-lever unit for safe travel, the decision for it followed as a matter of course. There was a vacuum gearshift option for '39 too, and new styling again, this time courtesy completely of Art and Colour.

Chevrolet remained number one.

Variations on the theme for '40 included the three-quarters of an inch deleted on the '37 being returned to the Chevy wheelbase—for an even 113 inches again—and the Master DeLuxe being augmented by a new Special DeLuxe series at the top, which brought the Master DeLuxe down a peg to middle-of-the-line Chevrolet—with the Standard-cum-Master now the Master 85, the numerical figure added for a reason which apparently remained promotionally unexplained. It would seem likely to have indicated developed horsepower, though heretofore it had been eighty, and there was no advertising mention that it had been increased, nor engineering refinements to indicate that it might have been.*

Mention of horsepower was made in '41, when combustion chamber redesign boosted the figure to ninety. This negated any rationale for the previous designation of Master 85, and it was dropped, which meant the Master DeLuxe series was now Chevrolet's low-price leader. In the spring, the top-of-the-line Special DeLuxe was given a close-coupled Fleetline Sedan spin-off. The Chevrolet wheelbase was increased this year to 116 inches, and all Chevrolets now had Knee-Action.

Chevrolet remained number one.

Each year since 1937 had seen Chevrolet proceed from strength to strength. Was it only, in Marvin Coyle's words, luck and avoiding blunders? One can't say that luck—as the inimitable Mae West once observed about goodness—had "nothin' to do with it." Still, it seemed that Chevrolet, more importantly than not doing anything wrong, had done almost everything right.

But now everything was about to change. Chevrolet's 90 hp engine was advertised as the Victory Six. And it seemed to refer to more than Chevrolet's by-now annual winning of the sales race. The cars for 1942 were modified only superficially from '41. And they wouldn't be built for long.

---

*Whatever the reason for the designation, the Master 85 shall ever be remembered by students of motor sport as the vehicle with which the General Motors dealer in Balcarse, Argentina—a fellow by the name of Juan Mañuel Fangio—launched his competition career. With the support of General Motors of Argentina, he entered one of these cars in the gruelling 5900-mile Buenos Aires-Lima-Buenos Aires race and won it at an average of 53.6 mph. It was the first major race victory of countless others for the man who would become World Champion five times.

CHAPTER FIVE

TOWARD A NEW CHEVROLET IMAGE

The Postwar Finale of the Cast Iron Wonder

The 25,000,000th car to be produced by General Motors in its history had rolled off the assembly line in Flint on January 11th, 1940 at eleven o'clock in the morning. It was painted an appropriate silver and it was a Chevrolet.

That evening, at six-thirty, in the Masonic Temple in Detroit, there was a gala dinner to celebrate the significance of this, tossed by GM chairman of the board Alfred P. Sloan, Jr. and GM president William S. Knudsen. Attending were the general managers of all the divisions in General Motors, amongst high ranking corporate officials, other leaders in the automotive industry—and one industry has-been. Billy Durant was invited too.

Bygones at last were bygones. The man who founded General Motors and who, upon losing it the first time, started Chevrolet to get it back, was introduced by the man who inherited the wreck of General Motors when it was lost by its founder for the second time and who saved Chevrolet from oblivion. There was something beautifully poignant in this meeting of Mr. Durant and Mr. Sloan.

"Too often," said Alfred Sloan, "we fail to recognize the creative spirit so essential to start the enterprises that characterize American businesses and that have made our system the envy of the world." A short while later, Billy Durant mused, "I do wish Mr. Sloan, that you had known me when we were laying the foundation, when speed and action seemed necessary."

From that foundation in 1908, General Motors had become a colossus unprecedented in the industrial world; from its debut in 1912, Chevrolet had become the superstar of the GM show. The man who had created both was now running a bowling alley in Flint, and planning to open that city's first drive-in restaurant. In two years Durant would suffer a stroke; in five he would be dead.

Later that evening the silver Chevrolet that was the 25,000,000th car to be produced by General Motors was ceremonially sealed in a glass case; Charles F. Kettering, GM vice-president in charge of research, noted that this hermetic sealing guaranteed the car's preservation and therefore "theoretically" its value would not decrease in the future—though, because of the automobile developments to come, the car in the glass case "would actually be almost worthless except as a museum piece" in twenty years or so.

Thereafter the anniversary car went to New York for the World's Fair, and everybody at the dinner went home and got back to work the next day. There would be another Chevy at the World's Fair too, the one-millionth car produced for the 1940 model year.

How could anything go wrong when everything was going so right? But in Europe Adolf Hitler had invaded Poland in September 1939.

Initially, it seemed America might not be involved in the war, and it was business as usual at Chevrolet. About this time *Fortune* magazine observed that Marvin Coyle had what in many ways was the biggest job at General Motors. Chevrolet was the fulcrum upon which the corporation balanced. Significantly, of all the GM division managers at that gala dinner—Marvin Coyle of Chevrolet, Charles McCuen of Oldsmobile, Nicholas Dreystadt of Cadillac, Harlow Curtice of Buick, Harry Klingler of Pontiac—Marvin Coyle was the only one who was also a vice-president of the corporation. Interestingly, too, he was one of the least publicized executives in the industry, and easily the least flamboyant. He quietly oversaw things at Chevrolet, and sanguinely counted the figures that proclaimed Chevrolet number one.

Keeping Chevrolet number one was sales manager Bill Holler's self-appointed task—and he was convinced that Chevy would remain dominant only so long as he remained indomitable. In 1936 he had undergone an emergency appendectomy and his convalescence was reported to be "retarded by lack of physical resistance resulting from overwork over a long period." But after a short period he was back at the job which routinely rendered his associates "aghast" because it was "simply . . . beyond human endurance."

Thomas H. Keating

In 1940 Bill Holler outdid even himself in a "feat of physical and mental endurance" that the press likened to an odyssey Homer wouldn't have thought of. Certainly no one in the history of sales management had ever tried it before. For 156 consecutive days he traveled and talked, visiting forty-five zone offices and eleven other selected cities. He traveled 7,926 miles by plane, 13,336 by rail, for a total of 21,262; he presided at 45 dealer meetings, 33 banquets, 45 wholesale organization luncheons, 45 press conferences and 25 special meetings for a total of 193. One of his aides on the trip told him afterwards that he shook 10,679 hands and spoke for a grand total of 410 hours. Just keep those Chevies coming

off the line, Bill Holler said. His unofficial title as America's number one salesman was one nobody had the audacity to challenge.

That a challenge was facing Chevrolet now which would strain even Bill Holler's boisterous self-confidence became evident as the months of 1941 passed. In May the *Chevrolet Dealers News* illustrated a fleet of Chevy 4X4 Army trucks en route to Fort Benning, Georgia—and editorially warned that every Chevrolet dealer should work "on the defense of his business against a shortage of service personnel." In October, although Chevrolet had already signed numerous military contracts with the government, Bill Holler argued for the automobile industry that "a market of this size and scope certainly cannot be considered as non-essential."

In December Pearl Harbor changed everything.

A few months later Bill Holler, ever ready to meet a new challenge, was quoting the philosophy of John Locke ("the best way to come to truth is to examine things as they really are") and the hound-dog yarn of a good ol' boy from Missouri ("sitting on cockle burrs and howling won't get it")—and Marvin Coyle was moving Chevrolet into all-out military production with the self-assured and deliberate determination that was typical of him. The facts and figures he totted up now were of aircraft engines (more than 60,000), military trucks (nearly 500,000) and armor piercing shot and howitzer shells (by the millions).

If World War II could have been won by exuberance alone, Bill Holler might have guaranteed victory singlehandedly. Soon Chevrolet's citizen-patriots, as he began calling his dealers, were being told how the Chevrolet-built high-speed armored Staghound ("unique among wheeled weapons in this war") was spearheading the European invasion, and how Chevrolet's former Soap Box Derby winners were taking care of things in the Pacific.

The winning of the war was being seen to, an effort resulting in all-time peak levels of employment and wages. Naturally what peace would bring was also being considered throughout. Early in 1944 Chevrolet was making plans postulated on the assumed date for war's end. "It is understandable why we do not disclose [it]," Bill Holler said, but on that day (reading between the lines of his speech to dealers indicates it would have been sometime early summer 1945), six-and-a-half million people forced to junk their old cars "will be walking or riding the public transportation systems" and another nine-and-a-half million "will have cars panting their final gasps of operation." Both Marvin Coyle and Bill Holler were determined there would be plenty of Chevrolets for all those folks. What the cars would be, initially, was another matter.

As the hostilities continued, GM high command inaugurated a research program code-named Cadet for the development of a new, smaller and lighter economy car. In July of 1945, two months after V-E day, General Motors president Charles Wilson* announced that this unnamed car would be manufactured by Chevrolet and distributed through its dealers, but that it "would not be put into production until a considerable time after the end of the war with Japan."

---

*William Knudsen had meantime moved to Washington to help FDR with the war production effort.

1946 Fleetmaster Four-Door Sedan / Owner: W.H. Heinrich

1948 Fleetmaster Station Wagon / Owner: Robert L. Lintz

1948 Fleetmaster Cabri

/ Owner: Kenny Lister

V-J day arrived September 2nd, and history has since recorded the "considerable time" before a downsized and fuel-economical car would become a requisite priority for Chevrolet and the entire American industry. That the Cadet idea did not march into the marketplace during this period was largely a case of there being no maternal necessity for its invention. America was starved for cars. Anything with wheels was bound to sell. The cars of 1942 were quite sufficient for 1945.

Moreover, the new small Chevy was one predicated less on the appeal of operating economy (that fuel supplies were infinite was a comforting if fallacious assumption at the time) than initial low price. And apparently enthusiasm for the project was confined to corporate levels. A few months after the announcement of the car by GM president Wilson, in fact, *Business Week* noted that Chevrolet wasn't "thinking too hard" about the idea. Neither the division's general manager nor its general sales manager was keen on it. Marvin Coyle thought both the car and the risk unnecessary, especially after Bill Holler wondered aloud if enough "elbow room" existed in the price area between the Chevrolet-Ford-Plymouth range and the used car market. There were rumors that Ford was planning to try and find out. As it happened, the rumors would remain just that—but Chevrolet had already decided to let Ford do the exploration anyway. And convinced the GM hierarchy likewise. So, for the immediate future, Chevy went with the old and just called it new.

Marvin Coyle said the cars were "the most attractively styled models that Chevrolet has ever offered," a rare bit of blarney from a man usually known for his candor. All that contributed to his use of the superlative was a grille that had its center moulding removed and negligible contorting done to its overall configuration, reworked bumpers, emblems and nameplates—and a front fender deemed "decidedly different" because it now extended a little farther back into the front door. Perhaps chief engineer Jim Crawford had told his boss that numerous mechanical improvements had been incorporated as a result of wartime engineering development, because Marvin Coyle initially mentioned this too. But when he couldn't find out what the improvements were, the new Chevy was thereafter advertised as sporting "America's most thoroughly proved car engine." The Cast Iron Wonder remained the tried and true 216.5-cubic-inch six developing a pleasantly adequate 90 bhp at 3300 rpm. Most conspicuously new were the names of the new models—the easiest of changes, naturally. The Master Series of 1942 became the Stylemaster Series for 1946, the DeLuxe Series metamorphosed into the Fleetmaster. The Fleetline had been a relatively new designation before the war, with the fastback Aerosedan body style introduced only in 1942, so no change was regarded necessary there.

The Ford Motor Company spearheaded the postwar production car drive, its first cars coming off the line nearly three months before the Chevies began rolling on October 3rd, 1945. This head start gave Ford first place in the industry that December (34,439 units to 12,776), but Chevrolet, its union problems temporarily solved, would quickly catch up and pass in 1946. And passed, too, would be the reins of the Chevrolet command.

The war had proved a Brobdingnagian effort for the division, and the coming of peace found the Chevy men who had led it ready for retirement or the advancement frequently preceding same. Marvin Coyle left Chevrolet as quietly as he had entered, for an executive vice-presidency initially, then he retired to read a little more Francis Bacon, to play a little more golf. Bill Holler said he'd be tak-

ing things easier in Florida. Perhaps. But he decided to write *Step Out and Sell* ("I never sold a car in my life, I always let my customers buy them") and book sales were 100,000 in four months. Chief engineer Jim Crawford moved up to GM vice-president in charge of engineering in 1947, but he retired too, four years later, to return to the career he had postponed in 1909 to get into the automobile business. At his farewell party, Jim Crawford was presented a set of brushes, an easel and a smock—and the engineer became an artist once again.

Heading Chevrolet now was Nicholas Dreystadt, who moved over from the general managership of Cadillac. One of his associates there remembered him as "a real hustler, tough, and didn't make many friends." The last was not surprising, since he had arrived at Cadillac in the depths of the Great Depression, and immediately began cutting costs and effecting manufacturing economies, something Cadillac people had never had to worry about during the salad days. "Nick made us look closely at everything. . . ," Cadillac chief engineer Ernest Seaholm later reminisced to historian Maurice D. Hendry, "Packard cut costs too, but they didn't do as good a job. They went down among the cats and dogs, and that cost them their name. . . . [Nick] did one of the most constructive jobs any man ever did at Cadillac." He was perfect for Chevrolet.

Taking Bill Holler's place was his assistant Thomas H. Keating. Though not as flamboyant as his predecessor, Tom Keating's credentials were impeccable: he had been a Chevy man for almost thirty years. Brooklyn born like Holler, he began as a record clerk in Chevrolet's New York City offices in 1917—soon after Billy Durant had used his new company to regain control of General Motors—and his loyalty to the marque had not wavered since. He stepped in as distributor in Tarrytown (New York) after the First World War, and therefrom stepped up through a variety of sales positions to the top one now in the division.

Chevrolet's new chief engineer was John G. Wood who had begun in the industry by helping several racetrack promoters in the engineering of a car called the Empire, which was produced until the promoters decided their Indianapolis Speedway was a better way to fame and fortune. Wood had joined Oldsmobile in the Twenties, become that division's chief engineer in the Thirties, and was now approaching sixty. It seemed apparent that the real dynamo in the Chevy engineering department would be big, ham-fisted Edward H. Kelley, who was appointed assistant chief engineer. He had been a Chevy man since 1928, joining General Motors first as a designer, then switching to engineering two years later. Under the tutelage of Jim Crawford, he had been largely responsible for the redesign of the Cast Iron Wonder in 1937. During World War II, he had served as chief engineer of the Chevrolet Aviation Division at Tonawanda, New York.

There wasn't an awful lot anyone at Chevrolet had to do immediately except see to it that as many cars as possible rolled off the assembly line. It was realized, of course, that old Chevies could not be sold as new ones forever; 1949 was selected as the model year for that matter to be taken care of and plans were being made accordingly. In the meantime, Raymond Loewy provided Studebaker with radical new styling and the automotive press with a genuine news story—while Tom Keating told reporters in '47 that not only had Chevrolet bypassed a shutdown for retooling but "on the day of the changeover, the first of the new models followed the last of the old on the assembly lines almost without a gap." The press reported this revelation breathlessly, but the real man-bites-dog story would have been that any shutdown had occurred at all.

Momentum scarcely need be lost when the only difference between model

Above: 1948 Fleetline Aerosedan / Owner: Jim Moloney

Below: 1950 Styleline De Luxe Convertible / Owner: James Schamp

1950 Fleetline Deluxe Four-Door / Owner: Jack and Dotty Robinson

1951 Deluxe Two-Door / Owner: John McAloon

1952 Deluxe Station Wagon / Owner: W.H. Heinrich

years was a yet-again reworked grille and the substitution of body and hood moulding by a creasing of stainless steel just beneath the windows. The editors of the British *Autocar* complained about excessive chromium plating ("cars with good body lines are often ruined by the flashiness of their frontal appearance") but Americans didn't mind. Tom Keating's problem was not selling but rather satisfying "the great number of waiting purchasers" who would have bought a Chevrolet if its grille had been made of gingerbread. Probably the most exciting assignments confronting Chevrolet's general sales manager during these years were his ceremonial duties in Akron for the annual running of the All-American Soap Box Derby and his role as honorary starter of the 500 in Indianapolis in 1948. The pace car that year, awarded afterwards to race winner Mauri Rose, was a dove-grey Chevrolet cabriolet. It was entirely stock, there being neither the time nor the rationale of needed sales promotion for the running up of a special pace car replica model.

By the end of 1948, production still had not caught up with demand, but the inadequate steel supplies which heretofore had seen the industry unable to produce at capacity were becoming adequate at last—and the time was obviously approaching when cars would have to be sold and not merely delivered. Chevrolet delivered 715,992 of its 1948 models. Amusingly, chief engineer Wood prefaced his advance data book for the 1948 Chevrolet with the "scarcely necessary" but "highly important" reminder to department heads that all information therein was strictly confidential. A reading of the document indicates there was little to be confidential about. Thin-wall babbit type precision main bearings were new, amongst a number of other detail refinements including a tailpipe that was round instead of oval at its end "to prevent exhaust gases from discoloring the rear bumper." The Chevy bowtie emblem was now placed on chrome-plated wings: "Interest is added to the straightforward design by raised horizontal beads which add depth to the upper portions of the wings." Comparatively, the new three-position ignition switch and one key to serve all locks was a revolutionary development. The stainless steel crease line moulding was a half-inch wider than in '47, and of course the division played around and came up with a new grille again.

The first brand-new postwar Chevrolet was slated for introduction at the Waldorf in New York City in January 1949. And there was great excitement at Chevrolet because at last the division had a new car to sell and, because America's appetite for any car at all was nearly satisfied, good promotion for any new one was paramount. Tom Keating would finally have a job to do. But he never had the chance to show what a good salesman he could be.

At this important juncture in Chevrolet's postwar history, tragedy intervened. In August 1948, Nick Dreystadt died of cancer. Quickly appointed to take his place was W.F. Armstrong, who had begun his career with the Remy Electric Company in his native Anderson, Indiana in 1912 and remained with the company as factory manager when it became the Delco-Remy division of General Motors. In 1925 he was production manager at Oldsmobile, in 1930 was brought to corporate headquarters as special assistant to then-vice-president Charles Wilson, and now was serving as vice-president in charge of the manufacturing and real estate staffs of General Motors.

Armstrong was not a Chevy man, and his appointment had the semblance of being a provisional one—which indeed it was, though it proved perhaps even more temporary than originally envisioned. Less than a year later, Armstrong

1952 Bel Air Deluxe / Owner: Tom and Nancy Force

fell ill and resigned. And Tom Keating stepped in. He had scarcely had time to enjoy selling the new Chevrolets, and now he was the major domo of the whole Chevy operation.

To take his place, Keating appointed William E. Fish. After an early career stint selling Packards in Pittsburgh, Fish had joined Chevrolet in 1931 as truck manager for that city; in 1933 he arrived in Detroit as assistant manager of the Chevrolet commercial car department and a month later was manager. Bill Fish knew trucks, and his record as head of the division's truck sales activities had resulted, in 1944, in the creation of a new post for him as assistant sales manager. Tom Keating was sure he could sell Chevy cars equally well.

Another assistant moved up at this time too. John Wood became executive assistant to the general manager for a year before retiring in 1950, and Ed Kelley took over as Chevrolet's chief engineer. This guaranteed an end to any clutter in the engineering department. Kelley's solution to running a complex operation was to take on problems one at a time. There was never more than a single sheet of paper on his desk at any given moment. "If you have more than one," he explained, "you get distracted."

For the moment, with the unfortunate distractions of the short period past behind them, the people at Chevrolet could at last get down to the business at hand. Prior to the arrival of the new cars at the Waldorf, teaser ads had proclaimed, "Some people will say . . . 'It has the sleek lines of a swift jet plane!' " and "Some people will say . . . 'It has the smart lines of a fast express cruiser!' " When the car arrived at the Waldorf, one reporter said it looked "like a small Cadillac without the fins." Which wasn't a bad review either.

Generally viewed as less boxy than the new Ford, less stubby than the new Plymouth, in styling the new Chevrolet was triumphant. Its wheelbase was an inch shorter (at 115 inches), but the car looked longer, and there was no doubt it was lower and wider. Chevy engineers claimed the lowering of the entire body (the passenger compartment was now cradled between the axles; rear-seat passengers previously rode over the rear axle) made for greater stability and, with the wider doors, provided easier entrance and egress—and that the greater glass area for thirty percent better visibility presented a marked safety factor. But Tom McCahill probably summed up the real rationale for all this when he noted in *Mechanix Illustrated* that "the new 1949 Chevrolet has been sexed up quite a bit." Glamour has cachet, and it usually costs more. Prior to the war, the highest priced Chevrolet was a tad over a thousand dollars, now the least expensive was several hundred dollars more than that—and the top-of-the-line cars passed two thousand. People may have noticed but they didn't care.

In 1949 Chevrolet sales passed the million mark for the first time since 1927, the year Henry Ford shut down his assembly line to change over from the Model T to the A and relinquished the number one spot in the industry to Chevrolet. Once Ford got his machinery back in gear, every year thereafter that Chevrolet

1952 Styleline Four-Door Sedan / Owner: W.H. Heinrich

retained number one represented a Chevy victory and not a Ford giveaway. Nineteen forty-nine was no exception.

The new Ford was all-new, even more so than the Chevrolet. After Henry Ford's death in 1947, Ford engineers at last were able to discard the antiquated transverse springs to which he had obstinately clung for years after independent front suspension had become the norm. (Naturally, Ford made no reference to "Knee Action" in mentioning its coil springing.) Ford's styling was all-new too, and the car had been introduced into the marketplace a full six months before Chevrolet. Conceivably, this had been too hasty, since myriad minor defects were immediately noticeable, most of them remediable for the model year following, except for the body which tended to leak rain and dust. "We are going to have to live in sin on this shell until we get the 1952 job out," Ford man Lou Crusoe told his regional sales managers.

Not that the new Chevrolet was beyond reproach. Its body didn't leak but it had a few eccentric noises, and its venerable Cast Iron Wonder was dubbed the "clatter and splash" engine by its detractors, and was widely regarded as less quiet than the Ford V-8. Still, the consensus seemed to be, in the words of the persnickety Consumer's Union, that "for all its faults," the Chevrolet was "the best all-round car per dollar in its group."

Interestingly, in a confidential comparative evaluation conducted by Chrysler Corporation engineers, the Chevrolet was viewed, unsurprisingly, as not the equal of the P-18 Plymouth from an engineering standpoint, but the difference in quality between the two cars was judged to be small, the Chevrolet was grudgingly conceded to have a number of features in which it excelled and the final verdict was that "the 1949 Chevrolet is an exceptionally fine automobile."

This exceptionally fine Chevrolet was offered in fourteen models, in two lines called Fleetline (fastback) and Styleline (bustleback), most body styles available in both DeLuxe and Special editions. All three of the competitors in the low-priced field did well in '49, and the variance among them followed traditional precedent. Plymouth sales were about half of Chevrolet's; the '49 Ford found its way into a quarter of a million fewer garages than did the Chevy. Dearborn didn't pass the million mark. At the Waldorf, Chevy engineers let slip to industry reporters, quite purposively, that their car's transmission would go automatic soon. Chevrolet was aiming to stay number one.

There seemed no reason to doubt that it would. Though it had been "sexed up," as Tom McCahill put it, "it's not dazzling. . . . America's No. 1 family car . . . is functional, reasonably tough and as utilitarian as a spittoon. . . . With proper care, [it] will last about the lifetime of a horse." What more might anyone ever desire from a Chevrolet?

For model year 1950, Chevrolet provided a little bit more. An even sexier Chevrolet model, which Tom McCahill had to admit "has plenty to offer in the flash division." Though he did cavil, in a typical McCahill metaphor, that "the greenhouse spread of glass in the rear is likely to make the back seat hotter than a Fourth of July fish fry in Georgia when the sun hits it just right," that was true, too, of the Riviera from Buick and the Coupe de Ville from Cadillac introduced the year previous. The convertible-cum-coupé was an idea whose time had come. Chevrolet's Bel Air was a beauty, the first hardtop in the low-priced field.

Powerglide was a first in the low-priced field too. And though Chevy engineers hadn't kept the secret well, Chevy publicists couldn't resist sending a couple of teasers to the press anyway. The first was a medallion embossed with a human foot, accompanied by the citation, "for distinguished service." The other was a small replica of a mattress which, the attached legend advised, was for resting that foot. "It took a little deep analysis but it finally came," said one of the few periodicals that published a reference to this publicity hokum. "Chevrolet was presenting the distinguished service award to the human left foot which can now be retired on pension since there is no clutch pedal to operate in connection with the 1950 model's automatic transmission."

Powerglide, optional on DeLuxe models, was based on a torque converter, more like Buick's Dynaflow than Oldsmobile's Hydramatic—and was another idea whose time had come. The American public was all for it. Like many plays or films, the automatic transmission became a hit despite the critics. In *Motor Trend*, Walt Woron said he definitely preferred a Chevrolet with conventional transmission, and Tom McCahill told *Mechanix Illustrated* readers that he would go down swinging on behalf of drivers who shifted for themselves.

A heftier engine was required for Powerglide, and chief engineer Kelley took the pragmatic route. The 235.5-cubic-inch Chevy truck engine was adapted for the purpose, putting out 105 bhp at 3600 rpm. The standard engine was beefed up as well, from 90 to 92 hp which Chrysler engineering spies said "is probably due to the adoption of a new carburetor [it was the Rochester B type earlier introduced on the Oldsmobile Rocket engine] and larger exhaust valves." Chevrolet prided itself, incidentally, in having the only engine in the low-priced field with hydraulic valve lifters. Amusingly, in an advertisement published that year, Chevrolet boasted: "In 1937, when the 216.5 cu. in. model was introduced, its maximum horsepower was 85. The improved 1950 engine, although there has been no increase in displacement, develops 92 horsepower—a gain of 8.2 percent!" This may not have been the first reference ever to a horsepower race, but it was a rather droll foretelling of the one to come.

For now, at Chevrolet, the only race that mattered was the one for sales, and Chevrolet won that handily in 1950. In April Tom Keating and Bill Fish took a whirlwind, 10,500-mile trip of Chevy dealerships and predicted a banner year. It was. The better than a million-and-a-half Chevies sold broke all records—and soundly trounced Ford as well; Ford did, however, break the million mark.

Chevrolet would top a million for 1951, Ford wouldn't quite make it; for 1952, neither Chevrolet nor Ford would reach seven figures. Partly the reason was military production for the Korean War—in 1951 Chevrolet had received its largest single military contract ever, for jet engines—and partly it was that the automobile market no longer belonged to the seller. There were more than enough cars available now, and the buyer had the pleasant option of being choosey.

The choice from Chevrolet for '51 wasn't much different from the choice for '50—and, on the face of it, there really wasn't much reason otherwise. The new self-energizing "Jumbo-Drum" brakes were claimed to be the biggest in the low-

priced field—and provided copywriters with sufficient new promotional material for advertising purposes. Advertising Powerglide with a vengeance remained a good idea, if only as a counter to Ford which was a Johnny-come-lately this year with Fordomatic. Calling the inevitable reworking of the radiator grille Chevrolet's "Fashion-Front" was perhaps less meritorious. Likewise—depending upon aesthetic viewpoint—the gentle raising of the Chevy's rear fender into what looked a bit like a tail fin.

By now Powerglide models had become available in Europe, and English road testers seemed considerably more enchanted with the automatic transmission idea than their American counterparts. *Autocar* found the Chevrolet version "does not suffer from the 'cause and effect' time lag which tends to exasperate the driver," and *Motor* enthused that "the smoothness of the whole process . . . is altogether delightful."

When John R. Bond bought a Bel Air, however, he got one with the standard three-speed. "The Technical Editor buys a Chevrolet! (oh, no . . .)," read the headline in *Road & Track*. Bond's last Chevy had been a 1940 model, and he was—as his readers knew—a rabid V-8 advocate. Defending his trade-in of a '49 Ford V-8 for the Bel Air with rationales of "I'm back to the people's choice" and "When Ford goes to ohv engines, I'll be back," Bond proceeded to like the Chevrolet for most of his column, "slow thru the gears, fast on hills; fair on gas, easy on oil; heavier than necessary, light on depreciation." His comparisons with the Ford generally favored the Chevy, but there was something ominously telling in his observation that comparing his 1951 Chevy with his 1940 Chevy (which he still possessed) was not difficult because they "show a remarkable degree of sameness." Especially in performance; zero to sixty was the same twenty seconds, the '51 was only seven miles an hour faster than the '40.

And so was the '52. It didn't look much different from the '51 either, nor the '50, nor the '49—which meant the styling was becoming old-hat. One critic, in fact, suggested the car might have been designed "by Herbert Hoover's haberdasher." Another said of its Cast Iron Wonder engine that it was "as up-to-date as red flannel underwear."

In 1952 Ford strode into the marketplace with a new six which was acclaimed as the "hot" car of the year, the one to beat—and company officials didn't bother denying rumors that an overhead valve V-8 was coming as soon as they could tool up for it. Pointed mention was now being made that "the last major revision of the Chevrolet engine took place in 1937." And rumors were few that anything new might be on the way. Even the staunchly conservative Consumer's Union archly offered Chevrolet as the best buy "for the driver who generally stays below 60 mph."

Nineteen fifty-three was a little better, in that it was a little different. The fastback body styles, never overwhelmingly popular anyway, were no more; now all Chevies had bustles, in three series: the One-Fifty (former Special), the Two-Ten* (former DeLuxe) and the Bel Air (now its own top-of-the-line series with two- and four-door sedans and a convertible added to the hardtop). The front windshield on all Chevies was undivided, the single piece of glass given a slight wraparound; the rear window wrapped too on all except the lowest-priced models. The 216.5-cubic-inch engine was gone; all Chevies were now powered by

*The designations derived from the traditional Chevy number codes, 1500 for Special series models, 2100 for DeLuxe. Bel Airs carried the 2400 series figure.

1953 Bel Air Sport Coupe / Owner: Jim Moloney

1953 Bel Air Conv

1954 Bel Air Two-Door Sedan / Owner: Harold B. Barker

the 235, with compression ratio raised from 6.6 to 7.1 to one and 108 hp for standard shift cars, from 6.7 to 7.5 to one and 115 hp for Powerglide models. The Powerglide engine was provided aluminum pistons, insert-type connecting rod bearings, and full pressure lubrication; the Powerglide transmission was given a new three-element torque converter and power shift.

Writing in *Popular Science*, Indianapolis 500 ace Wilbur Shaw reported how happy his "accelerator foot" was and how Chevy now has "a snap it was lacking" following all this major surgery. A Two-Ten sedan with Powerglide did win the Light Stock Class of the Mexican Road Race in '53, so there was no doubt the venerable Chevy six had been made peppier. But the winning car was a Powerglide model, with aluminum pistons, and it was no longer the Cast Iron Wonder. For model year '54, the changes incorporated in the Powerglide engine for '53 were adopted across the board—with compression for both Powerglide and standard units at 7.5 to one and horsepower 115 and 125 respectively. There was no reason to call any Chevy the Cast Iron Wonder any more.

In July 1953, Tom McCahill said that to him a Chevrolet looked like a "friendly old toothbrush." Half apologizing to his *Mechanix Illustrated* readers for the fact that he had not tested America's most popular car for some three years when, during that same period, he had tested several other makes several times, he offered as reason "my belief that a story telling you apples still taste like apples . . . isn't a story at all." And that, by a bushel and a peck (with apologies to Uncle Tom), was the real story. Everything that Chevrolet had been doing was a variation on the same old theme. When power steering was introduced as an option in '53—the first low-priced car to have it—it was promoted in ad headlines the likes of "See how many thoughtful things Chevrolet's done to make your everyday driving easier . . ." The Chevrolet had become very everyday.

And still it remained number one . . . despite a formidable assault by Ford, which was mounted on two fronts. The first was an old Henry Ford strategy: There was no such thing as overproduction, there was just underpromotion; when Model T sales languished, he simply flooded his dealers with more cars to sell. Some scientific law—physics perhaps—was violated in the process no doubt, but a certain advantage was gained. Now, when the Ford Motor Company tried the same thing, Chevrolet Division responded in kind—and dealers for both cars, with their showrooms packed, tried packing prices (raising factory list figures by $500, then declaring a $500 discount which, of course, was not one at all) and offering promotional gimmicks (a trip to Bermuda, a TV set, at least the ubiquitous toaster) to clear out the excess.

As the mid-Fifties approached, the Chevy-Ford race was neck-and-neck, and although a juggling of the figures would indicate a year or so too close to call, history has since generally recorded Chevrolet as the ultimate winner. Still, Ford was coming on strong, and in 1954 had a new overhead valve V-8, with a new body coming for '55. Clearly, something was needed from Chevrolet. It had already arrived. Chevy just wasn't letting on yet.

Early in 1952 GM president Charlie Wilson had told Tom Keating he could have anything or anyone he needed to breathe new life into Chevrolet. Keating said he'd take the engineer who had led in the development of Cadillac's short-stroke V-8 and who now was managing T-41 tank production at the division's gargantuan plant in Cleveland. Harlow Curtice, then executive vice-president, put in the phone call. "How soon do you want me to wrap things up in

Cleveland?" Ed Cole asked. "Just leave your keys on my desk as you go out," Red Curtice replied.

That took care of the anyone. The anything was already a full-size clay model styled by Harley Earl, and Chevrolet got that too. Actually, no other GM division showed much interest, but Ed Cole literally jumped up and down when he saw it. And so Chevrolet quickly engineered a chassis. When the show car debuted at the Waldorf in January of 1953, there were rumors it would be produced. One reporter, noting "the long-time GM policy against radical steps," said he'd believe that when he saw it. When the car did go into production six months later, Keating admitted it was to correct the impression that Chevrolet was "stodgy and massively resistant to change." The car was the Corvette.

Next came the Chevrolet itself. "You could get by on antiquated mechanical features as long as you had good styling," sales manager Bill Fish had observed. The Bel Air hardtop had been Tom Keating's pet, and its move into a prestige Chevrolet series of its own was at his insistence. "every car buyer wants his neighbor to know he's been successful," noted Ed Cole. Chevrolet's design studio was now headed by Clare MacKichan (who had taken over in 1952 from Ed Glowacke, chief stylist of the '49 cars), and it was MacKichan's assignment to style a new car that exuded success, and that had the panache, as MacKichan said, of "a young man's car." Chevrolet had been tending to forget a whole generation of potential customers.

There remained a good many six-cylinder adherents at Chevy who wanted, in one executive's words, "to sell against the whole industry." Perhaps Ed Kelley, who had seen to the last redesign of the Cast Iron Wonder in '37, was one of them—but now he would be taking his single sheet of paper to a new desk, that of general manager of manufacturing—and the production supervision (at which he would prove a wizard) of whatever new chief engineer Ed Cole wanted. Though there were other ideas floating 'round Chevy engineering at the time, Cole wanted nothing less than an ohv V-8. He had Tom Keating's unmitigated backing. And GM's Board chairman Alfred Sloan approved his plans without asking Cole to submit them. Cole tripled Chevy's engineering staff to 2900 engineers—and in just fifteen weeks Chevy had a new V-8. "We did not build a test model because there was not time to experiment," Cole said later. "That's how crazy and confident we were." Or, as Billy Durant had said of his founding of General Motors itself, "speed and action seemed necessary."

When the Chevrolet V-8 made its debut in late October 1954, *Business Week* noted that it had arrived at just the right time—not too early, not too late, precisely the correct "critical moment." How had Chevy done it? "Call it management judgment or call it luck," Tom Keating replied. Which was a variation on his predecessor Marvin Coyle's assessment of luck and avoiding blunders—because management judgment is frequently just that. And, dictionary definition aside, luck can be made as well as had, if the right people happen along at the time to make it.

An entirely new Chevrolet story began in 1955, and it began the same way the first one had. The dash and daring that created the marque also turned it around. Billy Durant's "best Prize Baby" had evolved into America's Number One family car. America's Number One family car, in the quarter century since 1955, has become many and varied Chevrolets. And every one of them, Corvettes to Camaros, rose from the solid base that had been laid for the quarter of a century previous, when Chevrolet was the Cast Iron Wonder.

CHAPTER SIX

THE CHEVROLET GETS YOUNGER

The Birth of the Great New V-8

The nineteen fifty-five Chevrolets had what many described as a "million dollar look." Company executives with access to the year's financial balance sheet might have been more likely to speak of the "three hundred million dollar look"—for that was the total cost of the effort to change Chevrolet's threadbare image to one that was fresh, vital and exciting.

But the spending did not stop there. When the new Chevrolets went on sale, Chevy dealers gave away 2,131,000 balloons, 1,016,920 bottles of Prince Matchabelli perfume and countless pencils, yardsticks, potholders, key cases and beanies. "With the help of all this razzle-dazzle," reported *Time* magazine, "Chevrolet Division Manager Tom Keating expects 20 million people to troop through his showrooms in the next few days."

In retrospect, only the introduction of Ford's Model A signaled a greater shift in the product mentality of U.S. auto consumers than the 1955 Chevrolet's debut. Overnight Chevrolet became a young man's car, fully in tune with the times. Clearly it was styling that had been the crucial factor. Chevrolet's general sales manager William E. Fish admitted that "I've never seen a study that said styling is the one thing that makes people buy—but we know it's true." GM chief Harlow Curtice agreed, saying: "We must 'create' used cars by bringing out new ones. But the new ones must not be too radical or they will not sell. Automobile owners are among the most conservative people in the world."

But Curtice's actions belied his stated respect for conservatism. After leaving the presidency of A.C. Spark Plug in October 1933 to become Buick's general manager, he led it out of its depression doldrums to a fourth place position in sales behind Chevrolet, Ford and Plymouth. Always the innovator, Curtice had mated Buick's lightest body with its most powerful engine to create the famed Century series, whose cars were capable of a hundred miles per hour. Later, as executive vice-president of General Motors, Curtice gave startling evidence of his recognition of the sales potential of new styling and performance developments. Two-tone color schemes, Buick's portholes and the panoramic windshield all underwent his scrutiny and obtained his blessing.

Curtice was a businessman who loved automobiles, one who tempered a tendency to brash enthusiasm with a rarely erring appreciation of what the market would and wouldn't accept. It would have been difficult to find an individual better qualified to preside over GM at the time when Chevrolet was shedding many of its old traditions and attempting to define new ones.

Given Curtice's inclinations, it was only natural that he would have followed the styling evolution of the 1955 Chevrolet, from its conception in June 1952 to the final debut, with what *Time* called "all the anxious looks a young father-to-be bestows on his wife." A horizontal crease in the trunk of a clay mock-up brought a disapproving shake of the head. "That's no good," he insisted, "you'll see that it casts a shadow on the bottom half of the lid. That shadow makes the car look higher and narrower. What we want is an automobile that looks wider." Curtice also saw to it that all the 1955 Chevrolets had a distinctive belt line dip, not just the two-door models as originally intended.

Curtice spoke affectionately of the new Chevy's "hound dog look," while other observers were quick to point out the Ferrari influence in the new front grille, a connection Harley Earl readily acknowledged. And was it pure coin-

Edward N. Cole

cidence that there seemed to be so many elements of Oldsmobile, Buick and Cadillac in the 1955 Chevrolet? Of course not; as insiders well knew, the new Chevy's close resemblance to its higher-priced siblings was the result of extensive deliberation and experimentation.

Chevrolet's earlier decision to delay the arrival of its rebodied cars from 1952 to 1953 created a situation potentially advantageous to Ford. Well-established on its three-year new model program, Ford could be expected to offer a new look in 1952, while Chevrolet would still be producing facelifts of older designs. In 1952 Chevrolet general manager Thomas Keating was well aware that the easy days of the seller's market were nearly over. In that climate, Chevy faced an intense Ford challenge with a dowdy image. As evidence of Ford's strength, Keating pointed to its superiority to Chevrolet in convertible and station wagon sales—both considered barometers of strength in the youth market. Harlow Curtice and other key members of GM management concurred with his assessment, and agreed that revolutionary styling was one important remedy.

Keating also managed to convince GM's Engineering Policy Committee that Chevrolet was "too six-cylinder minded." *Fortune* reported that the committee decided in December 1951 to "turn Chevrolet around." The stage was set for Ed Cole, who had worked on V-8 engines all his professional life, to lead a crash development program of the 265 cubic inch V-8.

Chevrolet, the overhead valve V-8 and Ed Cole represented the ideal harmony of product, power and talent. Chevrolet was eager for change, the V-8 was clearly the engine of the age and Ed Cole brought to both a level of experience equalled by few men in the industry. Cole had begun his career at Cadillac in 1930 and sixteen years later had become the division's chief engineer. He was both the designer of Cadillac's new postwar V-8 and one of the strongest proponents of the 1948 tail fins. When Cole had begun his work on the 265 cid V-8 in May 1952, a smaller V-8 had already been designed for Chevrolet, but Cole found its limited potential for growth, relatively heavy weight and high production cost unacceptable.

Both Cole and Harry Barr, a close associate from Cadillac, were delighted at the prospect of developing the new engine. Cole had worked on the Walker Bull Dog tank program during the Korean war and, "as a form of entertainment," had mapped out the design of a dream V-8 with his colleagues. "Barr and I were always fond of saying how we would do it if we could ever design a new engine," recalled Cole in the December 1956 issue of *Fortune*. "We knew we'd like a displacement of 265 cubic inches and that automatically established the bore and stroke." And in an interview published in the February 5th, 1957 edition of *The Wall Street Journal*, Cole added that "we ordered a plant and tools to build the engine before the engine actually fired the first time." The new engine would not be without its faults, however. Customers complained about its hearty appetite for oil and noisy rocker arms, but these problems were soon corrected.

Depending on their body type, the new Chevrolets were from 2.6 to 6.3 inches lower than their predecessors, and thus seemed longer than their 196 inches, a length unchanged from 1954. Harley Earl's staff had achieved not just a styling coup but a marketing masterpiece as well—a car that looked completely new, but was instantly identifiable as a Chevrolet.

Once a driver took his place behind the wheel of one of the new 1955 models, he would sense several less visible improvements. There was a new front suspension system incorporating "spherical" joints, coil springs and an anti-dive brake system patented by Maurice Olley. The length of the rear leaf springs was increased by nine inches over 1954; they were now fifty-eight inches long. In terms of handling, these changes placed Chevrolet at the forefront of American sedans.

It was not until the 1955 Daytona Speed Week that the extent of Cole's achievement was fully appreciated. Tom McCahill's earlier description of the Chevrolet V-8 as "the hottest car of this brand ever to race down the turnpike" was truthful enough, but told only part of the story. Chevrolet followed up the introduction of the new engine with a $59 "power pack" option which included a four-barrel carburetor, special air cleaner, intake manifold and dual exhausts. It was rated at 180 horsepower. In describing the "power pack"-equipped '55 Chevy in *Mechanix Illustrated*, McCahill spoke of a "wildcat—truly sensational." Its top speed was an impressive 112.87 miles per hour. In the acceleration trials for stock American cars, it took a respectable second place finish at 78.15 miles per hour against Cadillac's 80.42 miles per hour. These results prompted Uncle Tom to name the Chevrolet one of the "four biggest sensations of the week," putting Chevrolet into the same category as the Chrysler 300, Jaguar D-type and the Ford Thunderbird. Looking back at that breathless year, Bob Lund remembers: "The '55 Chevrolet with its V-8 engine did a great job of taking Chevrolet from being a relatively unexciting car from the standpoint of performance to a very exciting car in the mid-fifties and late fifties. . . . It was all brought about by the introduction of that V-8, which proved to be a tremendous asset to us."

It was indeed quite a year for Chevrolet. In NASCAR competition Chevrolet won thirteen of twenty-five short track events; in NHRA drag racing Chevrolet became the bane of its competitors, and what better was there to emphasize Chevrolet's new era than to have a red and white Bel Air convertible pace that year's Indianapolis 500? Despite this publicity Chevrolet didn't slack off. In June they began offering the Corvette's hot-cammed 195 horsepower V-8 for installation in any Chevrolet. Chevrolet also scored a coup over Ford with the Nomad station wagon. Lifting both the name and styling from one of the three Corvette-derived Motorama show cars of 1954, Harley Earl made it clear to Ford that it could not take its forty-two percent share of the station wagon market for granted.

1955 Bel Air Convertible / Owner: Stephen Styers

In the face of Chevrolet's onslaught, Ford simply refused to surrender. The fresh lines of the Thunderbird gave Ford's chief stylist Frank Hershey a good reference point for the development of the 1955 models and he made the most of it. Ford's clean designs, its modern V-8 and six-cylinder engines and the unique Crown Victoria model made for an impressive assemblage, but fell short of displacing Chevrolet's supremacy. Chevrolet's decision to go with a 265 cid V-8 for 1955 caught Ford, which had already planned to boost its V-8's displacement from 239 to 254 cubic inches, unprepared. And though Ford upped this to 272 cubic inches in time, Chevrolet had taken the decisive lead. Ford's "power-pack" V-8 was rated at 182 horsepower, but was barely able to keep pace in acceleration with a standard 162 horsepower Chevrolet V-8. A match with the 180 horsepower Chevrolet was nothing less than a mismatch.

In the showrooms, the sales race remained a close one. Chevrolet sold 1,646,-681 to Ford's 1,573,276. It was Chevrolet's best year ever, it was Ford's best year ever, it was the industry's best year on record. It would be difficult to repeat this success in the year to come with anything less than all-new cars. Nonetheless, both Ford and Chevy would give it a try. But this time around, the race wouldn't even be close; the winner in every way would be Chevrolet.

Having earned the reputation of being the "Hot One" in 1955, Chevrolet entered 1956 by proudly proclaiming "The Hot One's Even Hotter" and proceeding to prove it with a record run up Pikes Peak. Leading the Chevrolet engine lineup was the Super Turbo-Fire V-8 with a four-barrel carburetor, high-lift cam and a 9.25:1 compression ratio, resulting in a 205 horsepower output. All 1956 engines had hydraulic lifters—in 1955 manual transmission equipped V-8s had solid lifters. The "normal" Turbo-Fire V-8 was rated at 162 horsepower with manual transmission, 170 horsepower with the Powerglide option. The veteran "Blue Flame" six was offered only in a 8.0:1 compression ratio, with an output of 140 horsepower; the previous year its rating had been 123 horsepower with manual transmission and 136 horsepower with Powerglide.

The pre-production 1956 model, nicknamed the Monte Carlo (shades of things to come from Chevrolet), driven by Zora Arkus-Duntov at Pikes Peak, was camouflaged with plastic front fender covers and a zebra-like paint job. On hand to witness the occasion were NASCAR's Bill France and "Cannonball" Baker, the man whose 1929 19 minute, 12.8 second record Duntov was about to shatter. Duntov's 17 minute, 24.05 second run was only some three minutes slower than the absolute Pikes Peak record.

1955 Bel Air Two-Door Sedan / Owner: C.B. Johnson

But neither Ford, nor Plymouth for that matter, was willing to remain passive while Chevrolet piled one performance coup on top of another. Plymouth scored when it introduced its Fury just before the 1956 Daytona Speed Week. Although the 240 horsepower car wasn't eligible for actual Speed Week competition, Phil Walter's 124 mile per hour run on the beach in early February did not go unnoticed.

Both Ford and Chevrolet offered a 225 horsepower engine in time for the Daytona fray. Ford's was based upon the 312 cid V-8 used in the Thunderbird and Mercury, while Chevrolet adopted the 1956 Corvette's V-8 with dual four-barrel carburetors and the high-lift "Duntov" cam. Chevy outpaced Ford at Daytona, 121.33 miles per hour versus 118.13, but Ford edged out Chevrolet for the Pure Oil Manufacturer's Trophy, scoring 584 points to Chevrolet's 566. Later that year Ford was also the victor in NASCAR competition thanks to a strong 260 horsepower V-8. Of twenty-six Grand National races held after June 10th, 1956, Ford won eleven events while Chevrolet came away empty-handed.

Unfortunately, Ford's racing successes came too late in the year to alter substantially its 1956 sales battle with Chevy. That had been all but effectively settled when the two companies began restyling work on their 1956 models. Chevrolet's market research revealed several sources of discontent with the 1955 model's appearance. Surprisingly, its eggcrate grille had not been received with unanimous approval. Studies also showed that the majority of prospective customers wanted a more massive appearance. Chevrolet spent forty million dollars making certain its 1956 models wouldn't invite the same criticisms and succeeded admirably.

Ed Cole's uncanny automotive instinct once again served Chevrolet well. In July of 1956 he was named Chevrolet general manager, and from his new perspective he was pleased with what he saw. "If I felt any better about our program, I think I'd blow up" was how he buoyantly assessed the situation. Yet the sales success of the 1956 models did not come without intense effort from Cole and his team. "He tells the story," reported *The Wall Street Journal*, "of waking up one cold November Sunday and having a 'gut feeling' that 'we hadn't done the right thing' in designing the 1956 Chevrolet—despite the fact that the introduction of the car was less than a year away and all the engineering work had already been finished and approved. In any case, after getting the necessary approval from the top, 'we redesigned the car in eleven days and the next year we outsold Ford by 204,000.' " Clearly a man aiming for GM's top management position could not afford to be complacent. In August of 1956 Cole insisted that "you've got to go full-throttle in this business just to keep up. If we have to supercharge a bit, we can."

In speaking of the 1955 model, *Motor Life* had noted: "To Americans who have always liked GM's psychology that the Chevrolet is just a small Olds, this year's model will go a long way toward carrying that belief to full fruition." *Motor Life* was somewhat off target, since a more valid argument could be made that Cadillac, not Oldsmobile, had been Chevrolet's inspiration. In any event, Chevrolet vigorously applied their up-market philosophy to the 1956 models. A million dollars was spent to give their front fenders "the Cadillac flat look" and lengthen their hoods by four inches. A new full-width grille plus Buick-like taillights finished off a most effective restyling effort.

By contrast, Ford appeared to have stood still. Whereas the 1956 Chevrolet looked new, the Ford was painfully familiar. The December 1956 issue of

1956 Bel Air Convertible / Owner: Clifford J. Grunert

Fortune reported: "The result was summarized by Chevy and Ford dealers in the same western city. Chevy dealer: 'We got better in 1956, they stayed the way they were.' Ford dealer: 'Chevrolet made more of a change in '56 than Ford did. Ford didn't give the public a different enough car. A guy driving a '55 Ford didn't see any point in trading it in for a '56.' "

Admirable as its intentions were, Ford's aggressive pro-safety campaign didn't help its cause. While Ford stressed the benefits of its crash research program, Chevrolet blended safety into its performance emphasis. A typical Chevrolet ad described the '56 Chevy as a car that "loves to go . . . and looks it," a car with "frisky new power . . . to make the going sweeter and the passing safer." Chevrolet asked readers to remember that "this is the car that set a new record for the Pikes Peak run. And the car that can take that tough and twisting climb in record time is bound to make your driving *safer* and more fun" [emphasis added]. There were many other subtle ways in which Chevy pushed its fun-to-drive image. For one thing, it claimed to pamper the driver, giving him a seating position which, according to the March 1956 issue of *Motor Life*, "more approximates that of sports car machinery than any competitive passenger car make out of Detroit."

It was evident from the earliest sales reports that Chevy's way was the winning way. Paying no attention to the twenty-seven percent sales decline affecting the industry as a whole, Chevrolet's sales at mid-year totalled 805,100, up respectably from the 1955 mark of 756,317. With Chevrolet outselling Ford by an average of over 20,000 cars per month, Ford's advertising director Edward Rothman conceded that safety "does not appear to create an emotional urge to buy."

Cole attributed Chevrolet's success to improved product quality, more

1956 Bel Air Nomad Station Wagon / Owner: Gene Smith

aggressive selling by dealers and "thought-provoking" advertising. In just two years Chevy had not only repelled a determined Ford offensive, but had also tightened its grip upon first place in the industry. Twenty-six percent of all American cars in 1956 were Chevrolets, and *Fortune* estimated that if Chevrolet split off from General Motors, its sales volume would still rank either fifth or sixth among all American corporations, ahead of duPont and Bethlehem Steel and not far behind General Electric.

Chevrolet hadn't been able to maintain its record-breaking sales pace for the entire year, but its output of 1,621,005 automobiles surpassed Ford's by a comfortable margin of over 247,000 units. Even so, a rerun of this Ford rout during the following year was unlikely. Ford committed $400 million to achieve two objectives in 1957. The first was the familiar "Beat Chevrolet." The second was a response to the rise of Buick, which had already pushed past Plymouth to move into the industry's number three sales slot, becoming a serious challenger to Ford.

What was needed to achieve these objectives was "a new kind of Ford," and the '57s were admirably suited to that need. The Fairlane label no longer signified just the top-of-the-line Ford series, but was applied to all Fords with 118 inch wheelbases (the wheelbase of the lesser Ford models was 116 inches), and an overall length of 207.7 inches, an increase of more than nine inches from the previous year. Beyond that, the Fairlanes were also offered in "500" versions that had distinctive gold anodized aluminum side trim reflecting the influence of Buick's famous side sweep. While Chevy fans could point to the Ford grille as a plagiarized version of that used on the 1956 Chevrolet, there was no denying that the overall result was very effective. Ford also attracted considerable attention, most of it favorable, with its Skyliner retractable hardtop and Ranchero pickup.

The '57 Ford's good looks were at least matched by the appearance of the new Plymouths. With fins, torsion bar suspension and the special 290 horsepower Fury, Plymouth might not have been in a position to become number one in sales, but it was likely to weaken Chevrolet's ability to stave off the Ford offensive by penetrating traditional Chevrolet territory.

Maintaining a brave front, Ed Cole proclaimed that "it will take more than styling to sell cars [in 1957]." "You've got to get off the canvas before you can start swinging" was his response to the Ford challenge. Cole was determined from the first to hit Ford with everything Chevrolet could muster. His judgement of automobile styling was as keen as his engineering insight and *Fortune* noted that Harley Earl considered Cole "one of the best 'shoppers' among executives when it comes to deriving the last ounce of benefit from GM's Central Styling staff."

Without a "clean sheet of paper" for 1957, Chevrolet's stylists didn't have the same freedom enjoyed by their Ford and Plymouth counterparts, but when the designers were finished it hardly seemed to matter. The February 1957 issue of *Motor Life* concluded that "the overall effect is undeniably good, the car looks better than ever." Chevrolet's wheelbase of 115 inches was shorter than either Ford's or Plymouth's, but its new tail fins and front end stretched the overall length to 202.8 inches (up from 197.5 inches in 1956); use of fourteen-inch wheels led to a slight reduction in height.

Even if Chevrolet wasn't the styling leader for 1957, it didn't lose by much. And if the desires of modern day collectors represent the last word on the subject, then perhaps Chevrolet was the real winner after all. In Detroit, the firm of

1957 Corvette / Owner: Ron Weidner

Allender & Company found the 1957 Chevrolet an appropriate subject for a custom model called the "El Morocco." Based on the standard 210 Series sport coupe and the Bel Air convertible, the car featured a shaved hood, eggcrate grille and spoke-type hubcaps, all reminiscent of the Cadillac Eldorado Brougham of the same year and suggesting once again that Chevrolet was indeed a "little Cadillac."

In performance there was neither a need nor a desire for anyone at Chevrolet to suggest that their car was a copy of some other product. Chevrolet didn't have a retractable hardtop or a Ranchero-type pickup for 1957, but it did have fuel injection and with it Chevrolet could announce that it had achieved the "engineer's dream" of one horsepower per cubic inch of displacement from a production engine. "Every competitive field," said Chevrolet, "has certain magic milestones. In track, the four minute mile. In aviation, the sound barrier. In mountain climbing, the ascent of Everest . . . and so on. In American automobile engineering the milestone is this: one horsepower from every cubic inch of displacement." That was a language virtually everyone understood and with 283 cubic inches coming from a bore increased from 3.75 inches to 3.875 inches, it translated into 283 horsepower. Other 283 V-8s were offered with ratings of 185, 220, 245 and 250 horsepower. The original 265 cid 162 horsepower V-8 was continued only for manual transmission Chevrolets with or without overdrive.

It was also in 1957 that the fledgling Corvette came into its own. The disappointing performance of the original six prompted the installation of the 265 in late 1955. With the appearance of the Rochester Ram-Jet fuel-injected 283 horsepower 283 V-8 and a new four-speed gearbox in 1957, the Corvette was transformed. In August 1957 *Road & Track* called the engine "an absolute jewel, quiet and remarkably docile," but found it capable of propelling the 3000-pound car to sixty miles per hour in 5.7 seconds.

Chevrolet's strong performance image, coupled with good styling, a standard of assembly superior to both Ford and Plymouth, and its new three-speed Turboglide transmission (Powerglide was still offered) took it to a production dead heat with Ford. Most industry analysts concede the victory to Ford, but by a margin as small as 141 cars. In new car registrations, Ford appears considerably stronger: 1,561,883 to Chevrolet's 1,433,832. Apparently both were up to the tricks of 1954 in order to come away the sales champion. (For more information on the history of Chevrolet's 1955-57 models, see *Automobile Quarterly*, Volume XVII, Number 3.)

The year that followed, 1958, was not a happy one for the automobile industry. Chrysler Corporation, whose 1957 models appeared to come apart at the seams before their owners had paid for them, suffered dearly for its slip in quality control with a drop in output of some 700,000 vehicles. Ford was somewhat more lucky, but its revamping of the 1957 model line was badly fumbled. Across the country the allure of even longer, wider and heavier automobiles had gone sour and John Keats' immortal book *The Insolent Chariots* bore unwelcome testimony to Detroit's achievement of building the world's biggest, gaudiest cars in which the modern driver "crouches to crawl into an illuminated rolling cave, and then reclines on a sort of couch, there to push buttons and idly wonder what might lie in front of the glittering hood while the sun burns into the eyes through the slanted windshield that is overhead."

1957 El Morocco Brougham by Allender / Owner: Charles W. Davis

1958 Impala Two-Door Hardtop / Owner: Earl L. Van Antwerp

1959 Bel Air Two-Door Sedan / Owner: Nick McGraw

In another time and age the 1958 Chevrolets would have been sensational. They had a longer 117.5 inch wheelbase and nine inches more overall length. Their "dual-pod" front parking lights were inspired by the engine nacelles of the B-47 jet bomber. *Motor Life* believed the new Chevrolets conveyed the impression of "great heaviness," but given some of the other automotive excesses of the age, Chevrolet's appearance was reasonably restrained. Along with its new styling and size, Chevrolet also boasted of an all-coil spring suspension and X-frame which, like the 1957 Cadillac's, had no conventional side members. Two new Impalas, a sport coupe and a convertible, expanded Chevrolet's model lineup to sixteen cars.

The Impalas were not just knee-jerk reactions to Ford's Fairlane 500s. Their origin was pure Chevrolet. When the 1955's were reaching their final pre-production form, styling made a strong push to include an "Executive Coupe" in the Bel Air series. With small rear seats facing each other and squared-off roof lines, the coupe provided cramped accommodations for four, but the concept lingered on. Once Chevrolet designer Clare MacKichan and his staff began serious work on the shape of things to come in 1958, the idea resurfaced while the XP-100 show car scheduled for the 1956 Motorama was being completed. Though Chevrolet freely admitted that the Ghia-bodied 2.0-liter Fiat coupe influenced the Impala, the latter's low belt line, large window area and pillarless hardtop were advances over, not copies of, the Ghia example. *Motor Life* (March 1956) correctly depicted the Impala as sufficiently down to earth to arrive "on the streets within a year or two."

By creating the production Impala as a true four-seater (officially, however, it was marketed as a five-passenger), its stylists removed the severe profile that had helped torpedo the early Executive Coupe without losing its close-coupled effect. The old 210 and 150 lines gave way to Biscayne and Del Ray models with styling only slightly less voluptuous than the Impala's. Customers could, if they so desired, order Level-Air, Chevrolet's $115 air suspension option.

At one point in the planning of the 1958 models, Chevrolet had given serious consideration to the use of a spherically-shaped windshield. This had been so much of a sure thing that GM, not wanting to show its hand too soon, had scrapped plans to show it off on the 1956 Impala show car. But the bubble windshield's unexpectedly high manufacturing costs caused it to lose out in 1958 to the conventional panoramic version.

In reality, it was a switch of little consequence. Nineteen fifty-eight was not a year when customers were flocking to the showrooms with checkbook in hand. Despite Chevrolet's claim that "there's never been a model change to match this one," customers failed to respond to such new features as "flowing Sculpturamic styling" and a "Safety Girder Frame." Although the new Chevrolets looked more than ever like Cadillacs, the market for big cars had weakened and Detroit assembled only 4.2 million cars, down dramatically from 1955's record of 7.9 million. Chevrolet was also hard hit, its sales dropping to 1,233,477 units, down over 200,000 from 1957. Not since 1949 had Chevrolet dipped so close to the one million level.

Chevrolet's woes were compounded by the flat performance of its new 348 cid V-8. Weighing 110 pounds more than the 283 V-8, the 348 was intended to provide Chevrolet with an engine that was large enough to counter Ford's 352 cid "Interceptor Special" V-8 and also suitable for use in both its cars and trucks. On paper, the 280 horsepower Super Turbo-Thrust version with triple two-barrel carburetors and 9.5:1 compression ratio promised power, but it proved embarassingly inferior to the 283 in performance. At Daytona, for example, the fastest Chevrolet 348 was clocked at 126.249 miles per hour. The best of the 283s, with a speed of 131.004 miles per hour, had no difficulty in overcoming its big brother.

Not until mid-1958, when Chevrolet released its 348 "Law Enforcement Engine" to the public, was this state of affairs rectified. The new 348 was available in two forms: with triple carburetors and an output of 315 horsepower, or with a single four-barrel carburetor producing 300 horsepower. Both versions sported the Duntov cam, solid lifters, an 11.0:1 compression ratio and a link-up with Chevrolet's three-speed manual transmission. Acceleration time to sixty miles per hour was a matter of a mere seven seconds.

Chevrolet for 1959 suffered from what today might be called a delayed stress syndrome. The Chrysler "Forward Look" of 1957 represented more than just a personal triumph for Virgil Exner. For years General Motors had been the industry's styling leader, but that had come to a sudden halt in 1957. GM's major models had new bodies that year, but next to the fierce competition from Dodge, DeSoto and Chrysler, their appearance seemed less than inspired. It was a different matter in 1959, however; GM's effort to redesign all five automotive lines would strain its resources to the limit, but if the public wanted tail fins, then it would get them in abundance.

Everything seemed to be falling into place at Chevrolet until photographs of the opposition's upcoming models reached their ultimate destinations, in this case Chevrolet's Ed Cole and Ford Division head Robert McNamara. In each case, there was cause for concern, but for entirely different reasons. McNamara, who had opted to follow a relatively conservative path for 1959, feared that Chevrolet's flamboyant tail fins, huge rear windows (with seventy percent more surface area than the '58's) and exotic front end treatment would overwhelm his Fords. Meanwhile, Ed Cole, sensing that he had stepped too far ahead of public tastes, dispatched the 1959 Chevrolet on a series of public showings. The comments that came back weren't encouraging. Whereas Ford could confidently boast about the Gold Medal for Exceptional Styling that it won at the 1959 Brussels World's Fair, the new Chevrolet's styling was destined to be the target of humor. The 1959 model's exaggerated physical dimensions (80.8-inch width, 119-inch wheelbase and 210.9-inch overall length) invited criticism; its radical gull-winged rear deck became the inspiration for Charles Addams' famous *New Yorker* cartoon that pictured a small boy running from the family garage crying "Mama, something's eating my bicycle!" Among Ford partisans the 1959 Chevrolet was known as the "Martian Ground Chariot."

The Chevrolet's large front and rear windows gave it a light, airy appearance, but extending the back window high into the roofline gave passengers an unwelcomed opportunity to learn first-hand all they ever wanted to know about the greenhouse effect. Even traditional Chevrolet customers were probably a little reluctant to invest in the new car and virtually from introduction day Chevrolet offered incentives to help move out the 1959 models. Although Chevrolet won the calendar year sales race, Ford would win the model year battle, thanks to a steel strike that halted Chevrolet production in the fall of 1959. Ironically, six years later Chevrolet's general sales manager noted that the 1959 model eventually became a sought-after used car.

Chevrolet belatedly responded to Ford's Ranchero with the El Camino, which   125 it described as a "sedan pickup." Though its styling may also have been a bit extreme, *Motor Trend* (March 1959) named it "the best looking unusual body style," adding that its combination of "flat hood, thin roof, thin deckline and clean side spear gives it a look of motion at rest. . . . [It] adds a new form to function." Like other 1959 Chevrolets, the El Camino was available with either the faithful Blue Flame Six—now known as the "Hi-Thrift 6"—or one of Chevrolet's 283 and 348 cid V-8s that ranged in horsepower from 185 to 315. The 315 horsepower "Police Pursuit" engine, with triple two-barrel carburetors, 11.0:1 compression ratio, solid lifters and a long duration camshaft, kept Chevrolet at the forefront of America's high performance automobiles. Zero to sixty miles per hour required just over seven seconds and its top speed exceeded 135 miles per hour. A new addition to the option list was a four-speed manual transmission.

Despite its appearance, the 1959 Chevrolet's mechanical structure was decidedly down to earth. Though air suspension was still an option, Chevrolet remained conventional. In addition to a new anti-sway bar and anti-twist arm, a new rear crossmember gave the X-shaped frame greater rigidity.

In a comparison test of the full-size models, the February 1959 issue of *Motor Trend* named Plymouth as the best buy, saying: "We like it. Of the Big Three tested, this was the best performing and the best handling." Chevrolet, despite increased braking area and grooved brake drums, seemed a victim of its own unceasing facelifts. Said *Motor Trend:* "The buyer has no way of telling at this time whether this body style will be another one-year model or not."

The following year Chevrolet subtly toned down its appearance with more conventional front end styling and a squared-off rear deck. Yet with Ford offering what many auto industry analysts regarded as a very attractive car, there seemed to be a real chance that it might score another sales victory over Chevrolet. Fortunately it didn't turn out that way; the slope-nosed Ford ("The Anteater" in Chevrolet jargon) just didn't go over well with customers. While Chevrolet's sales grew by nearly 300,000 to a total of 1,696,925, Ford's slumped to 1,420,352.

Nineteen sixty also brought the introduction of Ford's Falcon model. Its hot sales record made it the most successful new car in history; against the mediocre record of the Corvair, there seemed no question about which car was the loser. But the Corvair-Falcon sales contest deserves a closer look. The Falcon's exceptional popularity came at the expense of full-size Fords, whose sales dropped by nearly forty percent from their 1959 levels. Quipped one Chevrolet official, "The Falcon chewed a hole in its own brothers." Meanwhile, sales of the full-size models remained steady over at Chevrolet. Thus Ed Cole's philosophy of designing a small car that appealed to a different segment of the market than the larger Chevrolet had been a success. Chevrolet's 1960 market share was a healthy 25.8 percent, and the following year, certainly not one of the industry's healthiest, it expanded to 27.2 percent.

Chevrolet's years of excess were nearly over; it was time for a refreshingly new approach to design and it was Ed Cole who set the tone for 1961. "Standard cars," he said, "will be shorter, higher and weigh less." Mechanically, changes for 1961 were decidedly modest, including such refinements as new tapered roller bearings for the front wheels. More importantly, the conservative trend signaled by the 1960 models was gaining momentum. The Chevrolet's new body, shorter and narrower by 1.5 inches and 2.4 inches respectively, carried only the

1959 Impala Convertible / Owner: William O. Chalk

127

slightest hint of yesterday's fins. Also absent (and not missed) was the panoramic windshield and its famous dogleg. It was replaced by a simpler, more practical design.

As the model year began, Chevrolet's top performance engine was the 350 horsepower 348 cid Super Turbo-Thrust V-8. Each valve of the high-speed, deep-breathing mechanical lifter system was fitted with dual springs. Along with the rocker arms, pushrods, pistons, connecting rods and the crankshaft, it was subjected both to the regular quality check and a second evaluation of material standards, surface finish and dimensional accuracy.

Though its triple two-barrel carburetors and either a three- or four-speed transmission made it a good performer, the 350 horsepower engine paled beside the first of Chevrolet's 409 V-8s, whose production began in January 1961. One of the first 409s off the assembly line shattered its opposition at the 1961 Winternationals drag racing championship at Pomona, California. Driven by Don Nicholson, it ran the quarter-mile in 13.59 seconds and finished at 105.88 miles per hour. And Nicholson's Chevy was capable of even more. The May 1961 issue of *Motor Life* reported an unofficial 13.19 second, 109.48 mile per hour run. With a 4.56:1 Positraction rear axle, the 409 was slower in the quarter mile (103 miles per hour in 13.9 seconds), but streaked from zero to sixty miles per hour in just 5.75 seconds.

128   *1960 Impala Two-Door Hardtop / Owners: Kenny and Pat Tucker*

1960 Corvair 500 Four-Door Sedan / Owner: A.M. Minton

The 409 V-8, rated at 360 horsepower, was derived from the older 348 engine, but used a different casting, a one-eighth-inch larger bore and a one-quarter-inch longer stroke. Its cam was described by *Motor Trend* September 1961 as "the most radical of any appearing in a Chevrolet product." The 409's aluminum intake manifold was similar to that used in the older 348 cid, 340 horsepower engine, with a single four-barrel Carter AFB carburetor.

Chevrolet followed the 409's impressive Pomona performance by offering a Super Sport option on any of its five Impala models. This included such extras as: power brakes and steering, sintered metallic brake linings, heavy duty springs and shocks, 7000 rpm tachometer and special Super Sport trim. Because Chevrolet intended the Super Sports to perform in a fashion that suited their appearance, there were no sixes or lukewarm eights available. Instead, customers could select from five power teams beginning with the 305 horsepower 348 cid V-8 linked to either the four-speed synchromesh or heavy-duty Powerglide transmissions. For those interested in even more power, Chevrolet offered the 348 cid V-8 340 and 350 horsepower versions, though these were available only with the four-speed manual gearbox. At the top of the list was the 360 horsepower 409, also available only with the four-speed. No matter what the engine choice, Chevrolet's description of the Super Sports' potential was a gutsy one: "the kind of car . . . that can only be appreciated by a man who understands, wants and won't settle for less than REAL driving excitement."

But the new Chevrolets, their new engines, their new look and the new SS option were just the beginning. There were more far-reaching and subtle changes taking place and Cole, at Chevrolet's 1961 new car press conference, hinted both at the new direction in which Chevrolet was headed and the uncertainty that lay ahead. "Whether or not in 1961 we will continue to have the same strength in the upper bracket that we had . . . in '59 or '60—particularly with the other manufacturers offering their smaller cars—is a good question," he said. "We don't know whether people will be just trading down into a smaller package. Or if we will be able to retain our traditional volume of sales in the regular size cars and get new business without new entries." With Ford's 1960 experience with the Falcon clearly in mind, Cole asked: "Will the sales of the new cars be really new business . . .? Will they come out of our hides—or some competitor's hide . . .? I don't think there is a single person today in our industry who can evaluate where this market is going."

But Cole had already made an educated guess. In the summer of 1960 he had given the green light to begin work on Chevrolet's "H-car" project. Its objective was the development of an automobile that combined "maximum functionalism with thrift," would be "economic to operate, maintain and purchase," and represent "good basic transportation for the average American family." It was intended to be a new Chevrolet as American as apple pie, developed around a formula that shunned such innovations as air-cooled, rear-mounted aluminum engines and embraced conventionality with an engine in the front, a high roofline and a large trunk.

But the Chevy II, as the new model was eventually called, manifested a split personality from the time of its conception. Developed simultaneously with a 120 horsepower 194 cid overhead valve six was a 90 horsepower, 153 cid four, the first from Chevrolet since 1928. The small price differential between the two engines, however, limited the four's popularity. Although a V-8 did not become a production option until 1964, Chevrolet designed special conversion kits that

1961 Impala SS 409 Sport Coupe / Owner: Floyd Garrett

1961 Impala Convertible / Owners: Jack and Dottie Robinson

allowed both dealers and owners to retrofit the Chevy II with the 170 horsepower 283 or any of the 250, 300 or 360 horsepower 327s. A car with the 360 horsepower fuel-injected Corvette 327 was tested in the March 1962 issue of *Hot Rod* and proved to be an impressive performer, zooming from zero to sixty miles per hour two seconds faster than a Corvette with the same engine. "With some chassis preparation and a good driver," wrote *Hot Rod*, "the V8-Two [sic] could be quite the Grand Touring sedan."

Other high performance extras were also available, ranging from metallic brake linings to a 3.36:1 Positraction rear axle and various heavy-duty suspension components, all reflecting Chevrolet's intention to offer a small compact that could be both practical and potent.

A fully performance-optioned Chevy II with the 360 horsepower Corvette engine was taken to England early in 1962 by Chuck Kelsey to campaign against the 3.8 liter Jaguars in British saloon racing. In his first race at Silverstone, Kelsey finished fifth, but two weeks later at Brands Hatch he prevailed and took first place. Said *The Autocar:* "An interesting situation arose when Charles Kelsey's Chevrolet Chevy 2 (sic) . . . beat three 3.8 litre Jaguars despite frequent attempts to overtake the 5½ litre 'sedan.' " The following year a six-cylinder Chevy II complete with racing stripes bettered forty-two cars, including a factory team of Ford Falcons, in the 1963 Shell 4000 Trans-Canada rally.

The Chevy II's engineering was a mixture of common sense and originality. Though its unit body construction was conventional, the Chevy IIs used a two-piece chassis arrangement in which the front section ahead of the cowl was a separate sub-frame attached to the main unit by fourteen bolts. Chevrolet claimed this provided a structure that was both lighter and stronger than a traditional chassis and frame arrangement. In a similar manner, the Chevy II's conventional coil spring and wishbone front suspension was balanced by a pair of single-leaf "Mono-plate" rear springs.

Chevrolet took no engineering shortcuts when it came to pre-production testing of the Chevy II. At the GM proving grounds, prototypes compiled 721,000 test miles. Both the four- and six-cylinder engines turned in an equivalent of nearly one million highway miles and the new rear spring design was subjected to the equivalent of 1.5 million miles of use in the laboratory.

In selecting the Chevy II for its 1962 Award for Engineering Excellence, *Car Life* echoed Chevrolet's original design objectives. "We think," it observed, "the Chevy II in either four- or six-cylinder form represents an important development in the American automotive field. We think it represents a return to sensibility in terms of basic transportation. It is a car of reasonable size, adequate performance and simple eloquence." Editor John Bond was impressed enough with the car to predict that it would be outselling the full-sized Chevrolet within two years and couldn't resist comparing it to his old sweetheart, the 1940 Chevrolet. There were remarkable similarities between the two cars; the wheelbase of the 1940 car was 113 inches, while the wheelbase of the Chevy II was 110 inches. In terms of power, the older car was rated at 85 horsepower, the Chevy II with the four at 90 horsepower. The newer car, of course, performed far better, was more economical and enjoyed obvious advantages in riding comfort and handling quality. These advancements seemed to underscore the Chevy II's claim to being a true Chevrolet and not an imitation of some other manufacturer's product. Said Chevrolet engineer Paul Prior, "The Chevy II . . ., while it may have been a little plain, was a real honest car. It was a good value." 133

CHAPTER SEVEN

CHEVROLET

THE SALES RACE

Chevrolet Takes Over the Sixties

Ed Cole left his post as Chevrolet's general manager late in 1961, replaced by Semon E. "Bunkie" Knudsen, formerly general manager at Pontiac. Knudsen, who had been appointed to the post in 1956, succeeded in giving Pontiac an aggressive new look. His removal of the sacrosanct "Silver Streaks" from the hood of the 1957 Pontiac just a month before production began was only one of the fruits of his zeal.

At Chevrolet that zeal continued. According to future Chevrolet general manager John DeLorean, Knudsen was so upset about the potential danger of the Corvair that he threatened to resign from GM unless the problem was corrected. The repair, reportedly, added only fifteen dollars to the cost of the car. After a fight that eventually reached the Fourteenth Floor, the floor in GM's Detroit headquarters where top management offices are located, Knudsen's request was granted.

Ed Cole, now in charge of General Motors' car and truck divisions, could derive an immense satisfaction from the condition of Chevrolet as it was handed over to Knudsen. In the supercar field its 409 cid V-8, soon to be immortalized in song and deed, made the Impala SS part of American performance folklore. Even if Pontiac was ruling the NASCAR circuits while Chevrolet engines blew up with embarrassing regularity, the 409 was an automobile to be reckoned with on the street. It was, said *Car Life*, "a car for the capable, responsible man who knows and appreciates finely tuned machinery. . . . It's just about as exciting an automobile as you can buy."

Chevrolet first offered the 409 during 1961 only to withdraw it after just a few had been sold. The marginal block thickness of the 348 made its expansion to 409 cubic inches both costly and difficult. When the 409 returned in 1962 it was substantially revised with a new block casting, high-chrome cast alloy heads, larger intake valves and a slightly lower—11.0:1 instead of 11.25:1— compression ratio. With a single four-barrel carburetor the 409 was rated at 380 horsepower. For all-out performance a twin four-barrel version, whose 409 horsepower at 6000 rpm recalled the engineer's dream of one horsepower per cubic inch, was available. With power like this at hand, no one paid much attention to the deletion of the triple two-barrel carburetor option.

Thanks to its extremely large 2.20 inch intake valves, wide ports and new high lift camshaft, the revamped 409 had little trouble exceeding its 409 horsepower rating. At the 1962 NHRA Nationals in Indianapolis, a 409 Chevrolet took Hayden Profitt to the Mr. Stock Eliminator title with a top run of 12.83 seconds at 113.92 miles per hour. Don Nicholson took his second Stock Eliminator trophy after his 409 managed a 12.84 second, 109.22 mile per hour win at the Pomona Winternationals. But even these victories didn't represent the ultimate expression of 409 performance. A Bel Air Sport Coupe equipped with a 409 horsepower engine, four-speed manual transmission and 4.56 positraction rear axle passed through the Pomona timing lights on June 2nd, 1962 in 12.22 seconds at 115 miles per hour. As tested by *Car Life* for its September 1962 issue, it accelerated from zero to sixty miles per hour in 4.0 seconds, from rest to one hundred miles per hour in 9.4 seconds!

At the other end of the spectrum, Chevrolet was doing what it had always done extremely well, providing basic, low-cost transportation. The down-to-earth Biscaynes and Bel Airs, powered by Chevrolet's no-nonsense 283 V-8, seemed destined to run forever. "As a workhorse it knows no peer," said *Car Life* about the engine. Except for their door panels, the full-sized Chevrolets boasted all-new sheetmetal. The results were subtle but effective; Chevy wasn't about to alter its winning face just for the sake of change. Perhaps the biggest styling news for the year was the Impala Sport Coupe's ribbed roofline, a flourish that gave it the look of a convertible.

Some housecleaning did take place in the year's model lineup. Slow sellers, such as the two-door Impala sedan, were dropped, as were the Nomad,

Semon E. "Bunkie" Knudsen

Parkward and Brookward station wagon labels. The Turboglide transmission also departed from the option list, leaving the revamped, eighty-five pound lighter Powerglide as Chevrolet's only automatic transmission.

Making its departure at the end of the 1962 model year was the curiously unpopular Corvair Lakewood wagon. Overall, sales of the Corvair were slipping. Despite the impressive performance of the turbocharged Monza series, sales fell from a 1961 high of 317,408 units to 293,561 in 1962.

Replacing the 348 in Chevrolet's performance catalog for 1962 was the soon-to-be-familiar 327 cid V-8. Derived from the 283 V-8—which was offered only in

a single 170 horsepower version for 1962—the 327's extra displacement came by virtue of a larger 4.0 inch bore and 3.25 inch stroke. The 327's 10.5:1 compression ratio, used on the 250 and 300 horsepower versions, demanded premium grade gasoline. Chevrolet's last link with the pre-performance era, the 235 cubic inch six, also made its last appearance in 1962. The following year it would be gone, replaced by a slightly smaller but more powerful 230 cubic inch unit.

Ed Cole, having orchestrated 1962's offerings, couldn't have read the market better. Chevrolet was in all the right slots with all the right cars; it paid off with a new sales record of 2.13 million cars and a 31.5 percent share of the market. Chevy's industry dominance had reached a spectacular high point.

Chevrolet's full-size 1963 models entered the year with a minor facelifting that included a new grille, straight rather than curved windshield pillar and a more horizontal, squared-off overall appearance. The Chevy II was only slightly restyled, but SS equipment was added to the convertible version. The most dramatic new shape for the year was the restyled Corvette. In both its convertible and fastback coupe forms, its production barely topped 21,000 units. When Chevy's total 1963 output was 2.35 million cars, it is easy to see why many regarded the Corvette solely as an "image" car.

Chevrolet's engine lineup saw several new entrants. A new base six cylinder engine was added, while the 283 V-8's output was boosted to 195 horsepower. In the 409 group the top engine sported dual four-barrel carburetors and was rated at 425 horsepower. A second version with single carburetor managed 400 horsepower. A third version, new for 1963, was a 340 horsepower 409. Termed the "police option" 409, *Car Life* spoke of it reverently: "Big and strong, with a smooth transmission and plenty of muscular horses up front, it begins to approach the ultimate in U.S. performance cars."

There were two additional engines, however, that never quite made it onto the 1963 option list. One was the famous Mark II "porcupine" 427, soon to become a legend on the NASCAR circuit. Since the 1957 AMA ban on manufacturer-supported racing, both GM and Ford had paid only lip service to the agreement. In 1961 and 1962 Chevrolet began work on an enlarged and modified version of a 409 that featured a specially designed valve train with staggered valves. By the time the car appeared at Daytona, rumors were flying about its more than 500 horsepower output. Vince Piggins, then head of Chevrolet's Product Performance Department, remembers that those prototypes sent to Daytona "proceeded to run off and hide from the competition." Then, while the car was undergoing development work to cure some valve gear problems, Chevrolet decided that it didn't want to be associated with this horsepower race and promptly withdrew the "mystery" cars. "It created quite a stir," continues Piggins. "We got the word from Mr. Cole to cease and desist and get all those people out of Daytona Beach."

Chevrolet's apprehensions about racing activity claimed another victim, RPO Z11. While the Mark II 427 engine was a specially engineered 427 for stock car racing, the Z11 427 was an outgrowth of the 348-409 series and was intended primarily for drag racing. Technically the Z11 was a "regular production option," available to the general public for a mere $1237.40, but only about one hundred Z11 packages were built.

1962 Bel Air 409 Sport Coupe / Owner: Rusty Symmes

1962 Impala SS 409 Sport Coupe / Owner: Floyd Garrett

1963 Corvette Sting Ray S

The Z11, which was based on the 1963 Impala Sport Coupe, was a true factory-built drag racer. In addition to the use of aluminum for the front fenders and both bumpers, Z11's were equipped with such performance features as a four-speed transmission, 4.11:1 Positraction rear axle, heavy-duty suspension and metallic brake linings. The Z11 427 was rated at 430 horsepower at 6000 rpm with twin four-barrel carburetors and 12.5:1 compression ratio.

At the beginning of the 1964 model year, Chevrolet's showroom success seemed destined to continue. The year got off to a good start with Chevrolet's victory in five out of six classes at the 1964 Pure Oil Performance Trials held at Daytona Beach. Putting in its first appearance at the Trials was Chevrolet's new Chevelle. A member of the A-body group that included the Oldsmobile F-85, Pontiac Tempest and Buick Special, the Chevelle was one outgrowth of GM's new Assembly Division, a department whose goal was to eliminate model proliferation by developing similar body styles for all divisions (except Cadillac) that shared common parts.

The Chevelle's 115-inch wheelbase was four inches shorter and 3.9 inches narrower than the full-size Chevrolet's, yet it came within one inch of matching the larger car's interior dimensions. In terms of engineering, the Chevelle's design was a straightforward one: perimeter-type frame, coil springs all around and a solid axle with four links. Three series of the Chevelle were offered: the top-of-the-line Malibu SS models, the regular Malibu series and the budget-priced 300 series.

1963 Chevy II Nova Convertible / Owner: Billy Joe Adams

1963 Bel Air Four-Door Sedan / Owner: Scott Kessler

1963 Impala 409 Four-Door Sedan / Owner: Jim Blaisdell

1963 Impala SS Z11 427 B F/X Racer / Owner: Bill Jenkins

1963 Impala Convertible / Owner: James F. Schussler

Chevelle engine choices were equally conventional, beginning with the Chevy II's 194 cid, 120 horsepower six. A larger 230 cid, 155 horsepower six was also available, while the 283 V-8 was offered in two versions, one with a two-barrel carburetor rated at 195 horsepower, another with a four-barrel carburetor rated at 220 horsepower. This latter version, which was also fitted with dual exhausts, was unique to the Chevelle in 1964.

"Everyone has a bit of swashbuckler in him," read a 1964 Chevelle SS brochure. "And one sure way to bring it out is to get behind the wheel of an all-new Malibu Super Sport." Chevelle's SS versions were available with electric tachometer, Positraction rear axle, sintered-metallic brake linings and a four-speed transmission. Along with the usual SS insignia and front bucket seats, Chevrolet offered the Chevelle SS in a Goldwood yellow finish not available on other models of the Chevelle. The trim size of the Chevelle station wagon made it an ideal platform for the return of the El Camino "sedan pickup," which had left the Chevrolet lineup after the 1960 model year. This was followed in December by the expansion of the Chevelle's engine options to include a pair of 327 V-8s with horsepower ratings of 250 and 300.

A January 1964 Chevelle SS road test by *Motor Trend* found the car capable but not inspiring. Quality control, especially in the fit of the body panels, was noticeably lax. Nonetheless, the crisp lines of the car appealed to American tastes. "If public interest is any indication," wrote *Motor Trend*, "there's a good market for the Chevelle. . . . It fills a gap in Chevrolet's extensive lineup and that's an accomplishment."

But the Chevelle's introduction did little to lessen the impact of several ominous problems late in 1964. On one front, Ford followed up its "Total Performance" advertising campaign with the new Mustang. Introduced in April 1964 as a mid-year model, it was an immediate sensation and defined an entirely new market. Mustang sales for the year crept dangerously close to those of the older Chevelle: 263,434 versus 315,269. Within GM itself, other divisions, jealous of Chevrolet's dominance of the market, began to intrude on traditional Chevrolet territory. Both Pontiac and Oldsmobile were able to increase their market share slightly in 1964. Meanwhile, total Chevrolet sales for the year (excluding 22,229 Corvettes) fell slightly to 2,119,683, the result of several year-end labor disputes. The Corvair alone, hard hit by the mid-1964 introduction of the Mustang, suffered a sales decline of over 50,000 units.

Chevrolet's 1965 lineup was intended as an antidote to 1964's year-end malaise. "More than in any year since 1955," wrote *Car Life* in March 1965, "Chevrolet has undergone significant change in its basic format." Chevrolet Division was equally immoderate in speaking about itself, saying that its lineup was "totally new for 1965." Areas of dramatic improvement included front suspension, rear axle, perimeter frame, semi-unit body construction and styling. The "Sweep-line" roof profile of the two-door hardtops provided the grace of a fastback without its bulky appearance, and wider front and rear tracks improved stability.

But quality construction, that traditional Chevrolet virtue, was often lacking in the '65 models. Writing in the November 1965 issue of *Car and Driver*, David E. Davis described 1965 as "the year when Ford built a car that was clearly better than the Chevrolet." The Impala "suffered from poor quality control and too many cost-cutting compromises in design . . .," said Davis, the result being the first Chevrolet in ten years that was really inferior to its Dearborn com-

1964 Impala SS Sport Coupe / Owner: Andy Lodi

petitor. "While Ford was getting tough," added Davis, "Chevrolet was getting soft."

Several Chevrolet partisans contested this verdict, among them Dave Holls, then in charge of three Chevrolet car design studios and one truck studio. "Nineteen sixty-five was, in my opinion, the most successful year for any design I know of. . . . That was one year that every GM car was a sensation from a Chevrolet to a Cadillac." In reality, however, Chevrolet was in little danger of being overtaken by Ford. In fifty-three years it had sold more than fifty-three million cars, with over twenty-six million sold since World War II. During 1965 Chevrolet outsold Ford by over 319,000 cars and on December 7th, 1965, became the first auto producer to build a total of three million vehicles in a calendar year. Bob Lund, then Chevrolet's assistant sales manager, recalls that "no car manufacturer, no division had ever sold three million cars and trucks in a single year. To me that was the greatest thrill I ever had, to break that barrier."

Despite this achievement, Chevrolet had trouble shaking off a "me too" image symbolized by the new Caprice that debuted at February's Chicago Auto

1964 Impala SS 409 Sport Coupe / Owner: Floyd Garrett

1965 Chevelle Malibu SS Convertible / Owner: Jimmy Morrison

Show. What *Business Week* described as a "Chevy with frosting" was also a Chevy-designed response to Ford's LTD, a model that had already been on the market for several months and represented eighteen percent of all Galaxie sales. While the Caprice was initially available only as a four-door hardtop, Knudsen left open the possibility of its eventual development into a separate series, noting, "If it is well received, we'll add another model."

The Caprice was fitted with the expected upgraded interior, simulated wood trim and softer body mountings, suspension bushings and shocks for a more comfortable ride. More important was the hottest of its three available engines, a 325 bhp, 396 cid version of the Mark II "porcupine" 427 used at Daytona. Chevy had not ceased development of the Mark II after GM banished it from stock car competition. For production purposes, this "Mark IV" 396 was a close copy of the Mark II, weighing 683 pounds without flywheel and clutch but after all its accessories had been installed. Its special heads were equipped with multi-angled studs, wedge-shaped combustion chambers and through-porting to give the 396 fine breathing characteristics.

In July of 1966 E.M. "Pete" Estes became general manager of Chevrolet, after leaving that position at Pontiac. That was the second time that he followed in the footsteps of Bunkie Knudsen; three and a half years earlier he had taken over Knudsen's post of general manager at Pontiac. During his tenure at Pontiac, Estes presided over a doubling of Pontiac sales, the refinement of Pontiac's youth image and the development of the GTO. (For more information on the development of the GTO, see *Automobile Quarterly* magazine, Volume XX, Number 4 and Volume XXI, Number 1).

He faced new hurdles at Chevrolet. When his rival, Ford general manager Peter Frey, was asked at a February 1966 press conference when Ford was going to beat Chevrolet, he responded, "Mr. Ford asked me that yesterday." Frey had previously described the onslaught on Chevrolet as a "somber, no-mirrors assignment—but attainable." Members of Ford's inner circle were confident that Chevrolet's almost 400,000 car lead could be halved in 1966, with a potential for sales leadership a year or two later.

Both Frey and Estes knew that the core of Chevy's strength consisted of two elements: the Impala and Chevrolet's 6500 dealers. "For anyone to beat us," Estes was quoted in the December 4th, 1965 issue of *Business Week*, "they will have to do it at the level of the regular Chevrolet." In 1965 Chevrolet had produced 1,821,262 full-size models, while Ford's output was 1,048,388 units. Chevy dealers sold more cars per agency, were better positioned to respond to demographic trends and enjoyed a far better relationship with the home office than did Ford dealers. Said one Ford dealer in *The New York Times Magazine* of May 1st, 1966, "Ford is still a long way behind as far as understandings between factory and dealer are concerned. If they have a dead horse, they try to shove it down your throats."

Overall, 1966 was a year of refinement for Chevrolet. As expected, the Caprice became a series unto itself, while all Chevelles received new outer body panels and trim. The Malibu series was expanded to include a four-door hardtop "Sport Sedan." The old Malibu SS models were replaced by Super Sport 396 hardtops and convertibles with the 325 horsepower 396 cid V-8 standard; 360 and 375 horsepower versions were optional. The Chevy II, which had enjoyed a strong sales revival in 1965, received its first major styling change. A new sloping roofline for the two-door hardtops imitated those of the full-size Chevrolet, while

1966 Impala Sport Coupe / Owner: W. H. Heinrich

its front fenders, hood and grille were more than slightly suggestive of the '55 Chevrolet's. In performance, Chevy II SS models moved into the same league as their big brothers thanks to RPO-L79, a 327 cid V-8 with hydraulic lifters that was rated at 350 horsepower.

Chevrolet was delighted to have *Car and Driver* depict the Caprice 427 as an unadulterated Cadillac, but Ford took the offensive with the "Quiet Man." This gentleman spent his days comparing the LTD's interior noise with that of some of the world's most expensive limousines. Chevrolet's Campbell-Ewald Agency responded with billboard scenes depicting a little girl asleep on the back seat of a Caprice. "The Shhhhhevolet Way," observed the caption.

Highlighting Chevrolet's efforts for 1967 were the Camaro's debut and the division's production of General Motors' 100 millionth automobile, a blue Caprice, on April 21st. The Corvair, continuing its slow slide to oblivion, remained unchanged, while both the Impala and Caprice received new rooflines, more curves and further chassis development. Overall, however, it was a lackluster year. Total sales sagged to just over 7.5 million, the lowest level since 1963. Although Chevrolet sales dipped to 1.98 million, their lowest level since 1961, its share of the market, after four consecutive years of decline, moved up to 26.1 percent from the 1966 level of 25.6 percent.

There were sound reasons for Chevrolet to be optimistic about 1968. A totally redesigned Corvette assured strength in the sports car field and the Chevelle received both a new body and a new chassis. The Caprice was hailed in the November 1967 issue of *Motor Trend*: "A spin in the '68 Caprice Sport served to remind us just how much of a squeeze the top models of the so-called low-priced cars are putting on high-priced models." But the real surprise for the year was the Chevy II with its new long hood/short deck styling. With increased interior space and a wide choice of engine options that included a lusty 295 horsepower 350 cid V-8 along with impressive handling capabilities, the new Chevy could once again touch the heartstrings of 1955 Chevrolet fans everywhere. It was an automobile capable of satisfying several demands in the market: "Nova," said Chevrolet, was "the great equalizer. The equal of cars known for their looks. The equal to cars known for their road-holding rides. The equal to cars known for their performance. The equal to cars known for their quietness." *Motor Trend* backed up Chevrolet's confidence in its new offspring by declaring the Chevy II to be its "compact car of the year."

1965 Impala SS Convertible / Owner: D. Bock

1967 Chevelle SS 396 Hardtop / Owner: J. Dumas

1968 Impala Convertible / Owner: W. H. Heinrich

1967 Camaro RS 350 Convertible / Owner: Dan Erickson

1968 Chevelle Malibu Sport Coupe / Owner: Jim Moloney

But as the sales picture for 1968 began to take shape, there was little room for rapture at Chevrolet as its market share resumed its decline, falling to 24.2 percent for the year. Things weren't much better in 1969. Sales held steady at 2.09 million and due to an overall decline in industry sales, Chevrolet's slice of the American pie crept up to 24.7 percent.

But this wasn't enough. Chevrolet was doing business in a fashion that was rapidly being outdated by changing automotive priorities and new challenges from overseas. Between 1967 and 1968, for example, imports of new cars from Japan more than doubled. Chevrolet's management had become bloated, overstructured and unable to react quickly when the need arose. A decision by marketing and advertising to promote the sales of the semi-comatose four-cylinder Nova, for instance, had been made without first consulting manufacturing, which, due to low demand, had mothballed most of the engine's manufacturing equipment.

There was also trouble brewing down in the dealerships. The men and the women who had for so long been the source of much of Chevrolet's strength in the marketplace were becoming restive over Chevrolet's lack of consistent quality control and the massive recalls that resulted. There were other worries: Ralph Nader's successful attack on the Corvair, Chevrolet's creeping loss of sales to Ford and increased competition from other GM divisions were taking their toll as well.

Thus it was a gloomy state of affairs at Chevrolet on February 1st, 1969, when John DeLorean's golf game at the Thunderbird Country Club in Palm Springs was interrupted by a phone call from GM group vice-president Roger Kyes. His message was desperately clear: DeLorean had been selected to succeed Pete Estes as Chevrolet's general manager. And he was late for work.

John DeLorean's lifestyle may have offended some occupants of General Motors' Fourteenth Floor, but his performance as Pontiac's general manager from 1965 to 1967 had been flawless. During those years Pontiac sales increased by twenty-nine percent, and though Plymouth and Ford dominated the NASCAR circuit, it was Pontiac that captured the hearts and minds of the street racers.

As Pontiac's chief engineer, DeLorean had served as general manager Bunkie Knudsen's "point man," the driving force behind the engineering and marketing innovations that transformed Pontiac into GM's most dynamic division. Knudsen once described him as "a fantastic product man and marketing analyst—one of the best engineers I know." DeLorean was very much an automotive renaissance man; at once an engineer, sales strategist and entrepreneur, he was far from the typical General Motors executive. Instead of adopting the conventional mores of Detroit automotive society, he shunned them, preferring instead the company of artists, musicians and other non-industrial, non-automotive personalities. Yet DeLorean's automotive acumen wasn't diminished by his iconoclastic personal life. On the contrary, he became more attuned to the market and was perhaps the best individual within the GM corporate structure to revitalize Chevrolet.

DeLorean moved quickly to energize Chevrolet with a fresh, new, demanding brand of leadership. His analysis of what needed to be done was simple and direct: "I regard it as my Number One priority," he said, "to improve Chevrolet's financial position. This means we have to sell more cars." Chevrolet had always been America's best-selling automobile, but the relatively stagnant 149 market structure of the postwar years had led to some complacency among management. Economist Paul McCracken of the University of Michigan's Graduate School of Business Administration once observed that a drop in sales brought sharply different reactions from Chevrolet and Ford. Writing in *The New York Times Magazine* (May 1st, 1966) he reported: "The Chevrolet people have been more sanguine in crisis. Back in 1961 I had lunch at General Motors and again at Ford only a week or so apart. The atmosphere in the GM dining room was: 'You've got to be philosophical. These air pockets come along. We'll get out of it. We always have. Relax!' "

Relaxation was not going to be on John DeLorean's agenda for a long time. Vowing that he would not return to the golf links until Chevrolet "hit thirty percent of the domestic market sales," DeLorean acted quickly to streamline a cumbersome administrative structure that clouded responsibility and slowed decision making. It didn't take long for the changes to be noticed. Said one ranking Chevrolet executive about DeLorean: "He makes a point of getting into every facet of the business. And decisions can be gotten from him promptly." At the same time, DeLorean encouraged more freedom of action for key personnel in the all-important areas of engineering and styling. "John lets us be very free," explained Alex Mair, Chevrolet's director of engineering, in the September 16th, 1971 issue of *Business Week*. "But he is ever pressing for innovations in anything from product to department reorganization."

The task of putting Chevrolet back on the track, however, involved more than administrative fine-tuning by DeLorean. Chevrolet had been slow in bringing new models and features to the marketplace; its quality control had often been inadequate and ineffective.

In terms of his freedom to attack these problems and strike out on bold new initiatives, DeLorean had far less maneuvering room than his predecessors. In the past Ed Cole and Pete Estes had guided Chevrolet by their own instincts. But in 1965 the General Motors Assembly Division, by combining Chevrolet factories with those of other divisions, reduced Chevrolet's freedom to respond to the market. *Business Week* reported that "Chevrolet found itself in the position of a customer and no longer able to freely control its production schedule and quality." The change was felt on two levels. Dealers often complained about not getting the right product mix to meet consumer demand, and customers often found that reliability and quality construction, long the cornerstones of Chevrolet's strength, increasingly fell short of former standards.

In 1970 and 1971 Chevrolet's malaise became a national issue when two potentially serious engineering defects led to the recall of millions of Chevrolets. The first, affecting 2.6 million vehicles, took place in January 1969 when the National Highway Transportation Safety Bureau (later NHTSA) found that improperly sealed rear quarter panels permitted exhaust gases to leak into the passenger compartment.

The second recall was more ominous. In October 1971 Doug Toms of NHTSA issued a warning to owners of 1965-1969 Chevrolet cars and trucks that their engine mounts could unexpectedly collapse, jamming the throttle in the open position. In its investigation, NHTSA revealed that approximately 500 owners had reported such mishaps, and suggested that there was "evidence that many more such failures have occurred," and that General Motors had allegedly replaced 100,000 engine mounts already.

Prior to the NHTSA action, Ralph Nader accused GM of closing, in June

1969 Chevy II Nova 114 Coupe / Owner: Chevrolet Motor Division

1970, an investigation into the motor mount problem without adequate explanation. Making matters even worse was Connecticut Governor Thomas Meskill's call for 1965 Chevrolet owners to check their cars for premature rusting. Faced with repeated charges from Ralph Nader and the federal government, GM was forced to accept the inevitable. On December 5th, 1971, it issued the largest automotive recall in history, affecting 6.7 million Chevrolets, Novas, Camaros and trucks with V-8 engines built from 1965 to 1969. GM steadfastly denied that the defective mounts were a hazard. Rather, it maintained that "publicity" had "generated a great deal of misinformation and misunderstanding on the part of Chevrolet owners which we are anxious to eliminate as soon as possible."

The recalls were hardly a good omen for the start of John DeLorean's tenure at Chevrolet. "When I got to Chevrolet in 1969," wrote DeLorean in his controversial autobiography *On a Clear Day You Can See General Motors*, "the reports [of recalls] were reaching crisis proportions." But the basic ingredients for Chevrolet's success were intact, just as they had been in the Fifties. Styling and engineering talent existed in abundance and GM had no intention of allowing the imports to increase their market share without a battle. On October 3rd, 1968 GM Chairman James Roche inaugurated the new General Motors building in New York by announcing that within two years GM would "build a small, economical, durable, safe, comfortable and well-styled car."

Closer in time, however, was a slightly less ambitious automobile, the Monte Carlo. Although designed prior to DeLorean's arrival at Chevrolet, it served as a fitting symbol of his objectives. At its press introduction, DeLorean stated that the Monte Carlo was to be "sort of the leader of the line.... Chevrolet's penetration of domestic industry has fallen from thirty-two percent to less than twenty-four percent last year. Our job is to restore the Division to its proper position. The strength of the Monte Carlo is our first big step in that direction."

Pete Estes had initiated the Monte Carlo project while he was Chevrolet general manager and though DeLorean was critical of some of the work under way in the Chevrolet studios, he had no misgivings about the Monte Carlo. "He thought it was a knock-out," remembers Dave Holls. This came as no surprise since the logic and motivation of Chevrolet's designers were consistent with DeLorean's basic goal for Chevrolet: sell more cars. Says Holls, "If ever you could increase sales at Chevrolet, it would have to be a car that would be an Eldorado-type car at a price maybe $350 and $400 more than a Chevrolet coupe." Once again, Chevrolet would be building its own Cadillac.

1969 Corvair Monza Sport Coupe Show Car / Owner: General Motors Design Staff

CHAPTER EIGHT

CHEVROLET

A FALLING STAR

The Costly Lesson of the Vega

The early Seventies were years of transition for Chevrolet. The musclecar boom that had reached its peak in 1970 deflated afterwards as the insurance companies, Federal Government and cost-conscious consumers realized that there was more to transportation than sheer horsepower. Until that time, however, Chevrolet's Chevelle, Camaro, Nova and Corvette models remained performance leaders in their respective fields. One 1970 offering was a Chevelle SS LS-6 454 that boasted an output of over 450 horsepower. In the same year a 375 horsepower 396 cid V-8 was shoehorned into a Nova. *Hot Rod,* in its July 1969 issue, found that this special Nova could turn the quarter mile in 13.69 seconds. "For the driver who knows what he's doing and likes to handle a potent car," said the magazine, "this little setup is definitely enjoyable."

Starting in 1967, Chevrolet increased the 327's displacement to 350 cubic inches exclusively for the Camaro SS 350. The following year, it was offered on the Nova SS and by 1970 a special version became available with the Corvette. Known as the LT-1, it featured solid lifters, a hot "Duntov" cam, 427-sized exhaust system and four-barrel carburetor; the engine was rated at 370 horsepower at 6000 rpm. The Corvette had traditionally been a testbed for Chevrolet's hottest engines and 1970 was no exception. The Mark IV 427, available since 1966, was increased to 454 cid in 1970. A special version of the engine, known as the LS-7, was planned for production and included in all of Chevrolet's publicity. The LS-7 featured an all-aluminum block, aluminum heads, and a solid-lifter camshaft. It was paired in the option listings with a new Chevrolet twin-disc ten-inch diameter clutch and the M-22 "rock crusher" transmission. Though planned as the highest output production Corvette ever produced, the LS-7 was killed off by GM's internal discouragement of cars with excessively high horsepower and also Chevrolet's campaign to weed out costly options that were clogging its assembly lines. This was known as the "de-pro" program, short for deproliferation and the LS-7 was "de-proed" into oblivion.

In late 1970 and into 1971, the brazen advertising of high horsepower figures gradually became a taboo. Though high-powered SS versions of both the Nova and the Chevelle continued to be offered, much of the best speed equipment, if available at all, was buried in the back of the option book. Hamstrung by a 1971 announcement by Ed Cole that all cars would operate on unleaded gasoline (in preparation for catalytic converters), horsepower and compression ratio figures dropped significantly. In spite of a 1971 GM policy shift to net, rather than gross, horsepower figures, the 1972 270 horsepower LS-5 454, available in the Corvette and the Chevelle, was a far cry from the great days of 1970.

Chevrolet's response to this transition was the XP-887, the "new small car" that Roche had spoken of in September 1968. Introduced in September 1970 as "The Little Car that Does Everything Well," the Vega was Chevrolet's most innovative automobile since the Corvair. Its 140 cu. in. SOHC four used an iron head with a block cast from a special lightweight aluminum/silicon alloy. The manufacturing techniques devised for the Vega used forty-three percent fewer parts than the full-sized Chevrolet because of its modular construction. Using new Unimate robots to perform ninety percent of its welds, it also involved the use of a new assembly plant in Lordstown, Ohio.

Chevrolet gave the construction of this $75 million facility top priority. Just days after Roche announced the new car, surveying of the site was underway. GM's willingness to pay high wages and the expense of overtime at the Lordstown plant was symbolic of its eagerness to begin Vega production. GM's vice-president of manufacturing, Frank Riley, explained in the September 1969 issue of *Fortune* that "the automobile business is not only seasonal but cyclical. The market changes rapidly. When we reach that stage when we have vehicles that will be ripe, you've got to move very fast to get that car out."

The Vega seemed to have everything needed to insure its success in the marketplace: a general manager supportive of its marketing, one of the industry's most advanced factories and a design in tune with the times. But almost from the beginning, the Vega's public image began to unravel. Only 23,000

Elliott M. "Pete" Estes and John Z. DeLorean

Vegas had been built when Chevrolet, along with other GM automotive divisions, was crippled by a major UAW strike. Experience with these early production Vegas revealed a number of design features in need of modification. While most were relatively minor, there were others, such as a poor-fitting gas cap which Chevrolet admitted could cause fuel to spill in "repetitive small quantities," and poor functioning of the Vega's windshield wipers and choke, that prompted a reaction from Chevrolet's old adversary, Ralph Nader. Chevrolet corrected these malfunctions when Vega output resumed after the strike settlement in December and informed owners of those Vegas already sold that their cars could receive identical "product improvements" free of charge at Chevrolet

dealers. This was not enough to satisfy Nader, who claimed GM was hiding the Vega's shortcomings behind the euphemistic term "product improvement."

General Motors had initially justified its action by maintaining that it was "inevitable as new cars get more and more usage and testing, that minor difficulties will sometimes develop. When they do, we fix them at the plant for current production and then we go to owners and have them fixed in the field before they develop any difficulties." When Nader charged that letters to Vega owners explaining this procedure failed to highlight their cars' safety problems, GM retorted that it had "determined these improvements didn't relate to motor vehicle safety, so it was unnecessary to follow statuatory owner notification procedure in conducting the campaign."

The import tide that had been rising steadily since the mid-Sixties was also reaching a crescendo in the early Seventies. Imports accounted for sixteen percent of all 1971 automobile sales and as much as forty percent in the bellwether Southern California market. President Nixon, acting under the mandate of the Economic Stabilization Act of 1970, announced on August 15, 1971 that he was imposing a series of wage and price controls that included the elimination of a seven percent excise tax on domestic automobile sales and a simultaneous introduction of a ten percent surcharge on imported automobiles. The result was an immediate and happy one for GM in general and Chevrolet in particular. "The Vega," wrote Fred Cray in *Chrome Colossus,* "$311 more costly than its major foreign competition, was in one neat stroke suddenly within $23 of the Volkswagen Beetle." Though the surcharge was repealed a few months later, currency revaluations effectively raised import prices anyway. Nonetheless, notes Cray, import sales dropped by only one percent and rebounded the following year. And although 1971 proved to be a 10.5 million unit production year, the industry's best yet, the ever increasing demand for imported automobiles, with their low price and high quality, was forecasting a bleak future for the Vega.

Though the Vega survived these initial assaults intact, serious problems remained. DeLorean's plans for the Vega to stem import sales had yet to be realized. In 1971, Volkswagen alone managed to outpace Vega sales by nearly half a million units. Yet DeLorean's optimism was still warranted, since Chevrolet was enjoying its best October sales in history and the rate for Vegas and Novas was on the upswing. The last thing the Vega needed was a second strike that would dry up inventories just as the spring sales season got underway.

On October 1st, 1971, the Lordstown plant welcomed a new manager, Alvin B. Anderson. Described by *The Wall Street Journal* as "toughminded," Anderson quickly got down to basics. "The plant hasn't lived up to expectations," he stated. "You can assume that just from the fact that new management was brought in." Anderson's arrival at Lordstown was much more than a management shift, since it accompanied the transfer of Chevrolet's assembly plants at Willow Run, St. Louis and Lordstown to General Motors Assembly Division control. No longer was Chevrolet in direct control of its own automobile assembly. Many reasons were given for this corporate-wide development, which left only four of GM's twenty-two assembly plants outside of GMAD's domain. Its advocates maintained that it eliminated costly parts duplication, provided GM with improved purchasing power and enabled the corporation to respond

1970 Nova SS 396 Two-Door Coupe / Owner: Floyd Garrett

1970 Monte Carlo Two-Door Hardtop / Owner: Jim Moloney

1970 Corvette Stingray LT-1 Convertible / Owners: Keith and Judy Brown

1970 Impala Four-Door Sport Sedan / Owner: Jim Moloney

more quickly to market changes. GM's critics suggested that this action, by divesting its automotive divisions of their own identities, would lessen the success of any future anti-trust action aimed at separating Chevrolet from GM.

Although Anderson's task at Lordstown was simple enough—to improve plant efficiency—his actions soon aroused the ire of the UAW local, whose membership's average age of twenty-five was the youngest in GM's unionized work force. Anderson's cadre of cost and production analysts found Lordstown's state-of-the-art equipment often unable to cope with the plant's maximum output of 100 cars per hour. These shortcomings were compounded by malfunctioning automated machinery. Unmanned spray guns, for example, did not always "remember" what body style they were painting and would waste paint by aiming their nozzles into empty space.

The elimination of several hundred jobs and what the UAW perceived as an intolerable line speed-up finally brought Anderson and the union to confrontation. GM maintained that it simply wanted "a fair day's work for a fair day's wage." Anderson regarded job eliminations and changes in expected work output as by-products of the plant's maturing into a viable assembly operation. "I agree that there are increases in the amount of work that some are doing," he said, "but in these cases it is overdue." Anderson's nemesis, twenty-eight year old Gary Brymer, Lordstown's union president, challenged his assertions, telling *The Wall Street Journal:* "This is the fastest assembly line in the world. A man has less than 40 seconds to do his job. If there's any featherbedding going on, I'd like to see it."

The situation rapidly deteriorated at Lordstown. By January 1972 five thousand labor grievances had been filed by the union, while General Motors charged that some workers had deliberately slowed Vega production by acts of sabotage and vandalism. On numerous occasions, the Vega repair yard was filled with faulty cars before an eight hour shift was half completed. GM maintained that these problems reduced Vega output by approximately 16,000 units and raised production costs at a time when the car was already priced higher than its major competitors.

On March 3rd, operations at Lordstown were halted when its 7700 workers went out on strike. This work stoppage, which many observers considered inevitable, came to an end three weeks later when a settlement that included the restoration of 150 jobs received a seventy percent ratification vote from the UAW.

Vega production had scarcely resumed when, in April 1972, the little car's reputation was again tarnished by the first of three major recalls. Owners of 1972 Vegas with the 110 hp engine—a total of 130,000 automobiles—were advised that in certain circumstances gasoline could spill out of their engines' carburetors. Barely a month later, on May 8th, an additional 350,000 Vegas were recalled for examination of a potentially defective bracket, that for the solenoid controlling engine speed. Although only five instances of this problem had been reported to GM, the recall of eighty-five percent of the 500,000 Vegas built wasn't the type of attention any auto manufacturer welcomed. In July came more bad news, a third recall involving 526,000 Vegas built before May 6th. The reason was not a design flaw, but the discovery that some Vega axles purchased from an outside producer were a fraction of an inch shorter than specified. This created the possibility of a rear wheel falling off, an event that GM admitted had occurred fifteen times.

1970 Chevelle SS 454 Two-Door Hardtop / Owner: Floyd Garrett

1970½ Camaro Rally Sport Coupe / Owner: Gary Witzenburg

Adding to Chevrolet's discomfort was a twelve page letter sent to GM Chairman Richard Gerstenberg by Ralph Nader's Center for Auto Safety containing a long list of allegations about the Vega's basic integrity. The Vega, it claimed, was a "sloppily crafted, unreliable and unsafe automobile," a car that "hardly set a good example in small car production for American industry."

There seemed to be no end to the Vega's woes. In May 1974 Chevrolet notified the approximately 1.3 million Vega owners that it would assume the cost of repairing any damages to their cars' engine caused by overheating. Until early 1973, Vegas had not been fitted with a radiator overflow tank. Loss of coolant would then cause the engine to overheat, raising the ire of Vega owners. Chevrolet's offer, described by *The Wall Street Journal* as a "potentially costly move," was valid for 50,000 miles and carried no time limit. In 1972 Chevrolet had provided a free coolant check and installation of the reservoir, but demurred in accepting responsibility for engine damages. The Center for Auto Safety had filed complaints with the Federal Trade Commission asking that Chevrolet assume both the cost of engine repairs and offer a five-year, 50,000 mile Vega engine guarantee. Chevrolet denied that this complaint had any effect upon its subsequent actions, which did include such a warranty. Chevrolet general manager Robert Lund said the guarantee was offered "to assure customers of the quality and durability of the 1975 four-cylinder Vega engine." Somewhat more candidly, a Chevrolet spokesman added: "We're trying to help the image of the Vega engine."

Although its reputation was indelibly marred by complaints about its noisy, shaky engine, rust-prone front fenders and poor fuel economy, by 1972 the Vega ranked second only to the Nova among Chevrolet models receiving the least number of customer complaints about quality. In addition, its 21.5 mpg rating in the EPA's mileage tests was the best showing of any American car.

Chevrolet described the 1976 Vega as an automobile "built to take it." Its "Dura-Built 140" engine carried a five year or 60,000 mile guarantee and a major advertising campaign publicized the Vega's successful completion of a 60,000 mile durability run in less than sixty days in and around Death Valley. Vince Piggins, who fostered the idea, remembers that when he tried to sell it to management, "they all told me I was crazy. And let's face it, it was a hell of a gamble, but we needed a gamble to pull us out of the position we were in." 157

The test, for the first 59,000 miles at least, was so successful that Chevrolet engineers idly wondered if the public would actually believe that the Vega could survive 60,000 miles with only a few cups of water added to the radiator. At 59,700 miles, however, one of the cars threw a timing belt. It was quickly repaired and all cars completed the test.

Unfortunately, this demonstration of strength came too late to save the Vega. Without emotion, Chevrolet trimmed the car from its lineup after the 1977 model run. The motives and rationale of the Vega's creator had been admirable, but their execution had been marked by one disaster after another.

These unmitigated miseries blocked the inclusion of several exotic versions into the Vega line. Lurking in the corners of various studios were Vegas with V-8 engines, convertible bodies, four-wheel drive and a pick-up version patterned after the El Camino. The most exciting of these prototype Vegas was the XP-898, a two-seater sports car. Its engine, modified to accept angled valves, hemispherical combustion chambers and a cross-flow cylinder head, developed 111 net horsepower at 6000 rpm, sufficient for a 114 mph top speed.

In spite of its checkered career, the Vega had one last chance at staging a comeback and making automotive history. Its claim to greatness was tied to GM president Ed Cole's burning desire to build a Wankel-powered automobile. Cole, who was immensely proud that GM had secured production rights to the Wankel for $50 million without any royalty obligations, was the engine's benevolent godfather at General Motors. Unlike the 1955 Chevrolet V-8, however, the Wankel program brought him very little satisfaction.

GM's plans for the Wankel went far beyond its use in the Vega, ultimately including a new generation of GM sedans, all Wankel powered, with front-wheel drive, compact dimensions and spacious interiors. GM moved cautiously toward their manufacture in the mid-Seventies, at least in its public statements. In February 1972, while willing to admit the Wankel program was advancing satisfactorily, GM chairman Richard Gerstenberg declined to commit GM to its production. "We don't know yet," he said, "whether the Wankel is the engine of the future. Its use in a production car is a 'big if.' "

Later, when Ed Cole was asked at GM's annual stockholder's meeting if a Wankel-powered Vega was planned for 1973, he answered with an unequivocal "no." This did little to cool speculation that a significant announcement about the Wankel would be forthcoming. Speculation was furthered in July, when Cole admitted that 1974 could bring a Vega-Wankel. After letters of commitment from General Motors to the Sealed Power and Dana Corporations for machinery to produce Wankel engines became public knowledge, Richard Gerstenberg issued a four-paragraph statement, saying, in part: "Wankel engine development and manufacturing processing work will continue, and if this progresses as anticipated, public introduction of the engine as an option in the Vega line may be made in about two years."

On the eve of his departure from Chevrolet's general managership in September 1972, John DeLorean was optimistic about the Wankel's prospects: "We think we have all the problems solved." This was the highpoint of the Wankel's fortunes at GM. DeLorean's successor, F. James McDonald, announced a year later at the 1974 new model press preview that Chevrolet's plans were essentially unchanged; it still expected to build from 165,000 to 200,000 Wankel-Vegas in the 1975 model year. But the fuel shortages in 1973-74 that gave the Vega its last sales spurt were also the Wankel's undoing. Ed Cole, who wanted to see the

1971 Monte Carlo SS 454 Two-Door Coupe / Owner: Marv Reis

Wankel become a reality before his retirement from the GM presidency, reported that the Wankel's 17.6 mpg average was competitive with that of conventional engines of equivalent displacement and horsepower. But Thomas R. Zimmer, GM staff engineer in charge of the Wankel project, conceded that "meeting the current and projected emission requirements while maintaining satisfactory fuel economy has—as expected—posed a very difficult challenge."

The Wankel project was barely alive when its originally scheduled fall 1974 debut came and went, but its advocates redirected their energies toward a 1975 production startup. In September 1974 McDonald forecast that a Wankel-engined Monza 2+2 whose emission certification would begin in October would be produced "late in the 1975 model year." A week later, on September 27th, 1974, General Motors, while declaring the Wankel neither "dead nor abandoned," announced its indefinite postponement. It was an embarrassment for McDonald, whose office reported that he hadn't known about the shelving when he made his earlier statement.

In one of his last formal actions as GM president, Ed Cole all but closed the book on the Wankel, stating: "Considerable progress has been made in the ongoing GM rotary-engine development program. The lack of relief from the very stringent 1977 standards, which we aren't sure can be achieved even with current production engines, made it especially impractical to put into production any new engine which doesn't presently have the potential to meet these standards." Even at this low point in the fate of the Wankel, Cole held true to his convictions, concluding: "The rotary engine, because of its size and weight, has important advantages, particularly as the automotive market continues to grow in the smaller size category." Two years later, in April 1979, after it had consumed tens of millions of dollars, General Motors announced all research and development work on the Wankel had ended. "It didn't demonstrate the potential for low emissions levels and fuel economy as did conventional engines," commented a spokesman.

Even before its introduction in 1971, another sort of potential had attracted Keith Duckworth of England's Cosworth Engineering to the Vega. Cosworth's Grand Prix V-8's had been powering the world's Formula One champions since

1971 Chevelle Malibu Convertible / Owner: Joe Guisti

1968 and it appeared to Duckworth that the Vega engine, destroked to a displacement of 121.7 cubic inches, offered similar prospects as a Formula Two racing powerplant. Although the Vega's competition record had not been impressive, Chevrolet Engineering kept close tabs on the Formula Two project. Veteran engine designer Calvin Wade made several visits to the Cosworth plant in Northampton and his enthusiasm for a production engine based on the Formula version was supported by both DeLorean and Cole. Early in 1971, with five Formula Two engines at its disposal, Chevrolet began work on the new engine, which Zora Arkus-Duntov would later describe as "the nicest four-cylinder I ever drove (sic)."

The specifications of the production Cosworth Vega engine seemed to insure the realization of DeLorean's goal of giving the Vega a GTO-like relationship with other Chevrolets. Its Duckworth-designed aluminum cylinder head was equipped with dual overhead camshafts and four valves per cylinder. A Bendix electronic fuel injection system was also fitted. Promises of 170 horsepower, a 122 mph top speed along with faster steering and improved handling created visions among motoring enthusiasts of an American version of the BMW 2002tii or Datsun 240Z. When Chevrolet presented its 1974 models to the press, a Cosworth Vega prototype was available for driving impressions. Although it

was afflicted with the Vega's engine-induced vibration and a powerplant downrated to 135 hp at 6400 rpm, the car's strong performance remained intact.

Chevrolet's goal of a 1974 debut for the Cosworth Vega was shattered when, in the midst of the required 50,000 mile emissions certification run, the engine suffered burned exhaust valves at the 40,000 mile mark. This spurred a major redesign of the fuel system, the use of a new high-energy ignition system and a special "Pulse-Air" air injection device that supplied fresh air to the exhaust system to help burn up pollutants.

The Cosworth Vega finally became a production reality in 1975, only to have its production terminated after just 3508 1975 and 1976 models had been manufactured. It was a handsome machine, available initially only in black with gold stripes but later in other colors, and was the most exciting Vega of all. But EPA emissions regulations reduced the performance of the Cosworth engine to a level little better than that of the original 110 hp SOHC Vega engine. Another factor in its demise was cost; list price for a 1976 Cosworth Vega was $6066, almost twice that of the standard Vega hatchback. "It was high priced and that really put it out of business," said Vince Piggins, Chevrolet's manager of Product Performance Engineering. "It was a good runner, but it was priced out of sight because of the cylinder head."

1972 Caprice Four-Door Sedan / Owner: Roy Ramsey

The lengthy gestation period of the Cosworth Vega and the frustrations of the Wankel project seemed to have destroyed Chevrolet's plans for a sporting version of the Vega. A nicely styled Vega-based hatchback sports coupe had been ready for the Wankel's debut, however. And although the Wankel was dead, this new car was needed as a response to Ford's new scaled-down Mustang II. No better reason was needed for resurrecting the old Monza label. If Jim Hall and Chevrolet had been able to come to terms, its name might have been "Chaparelle." But Hall's royalty cost of one dollar per car, later scaled down to a single $350,000 payment, wasn't acceptable to Chevrolet. The deadlock was of little importance, as the name Monza seemed suitable for the latest offering from Chevrolet's sports department.

The Monza shared the Vega's 97 inch wheelbase, but its outer body sheet metal was completely different. Also reducing the similarity between the two cars was the Monza's revamped front suspension, with longer coil springs, as well as a new rear suspension. The 87 hp (80 hp in California), four-cylinder engine with a two-barrel carburetor that was optional on the Vega served as the Monza's standard powerplant. A new 110 hp, 262 cid version of Chevrolet's traditional small block V-8 was optional. This engine, which Chevrolet advertised as the smallest V-8 it had ever produced, was a fuel-conscious performer, with

small valves and ports. And Chevrolet did not pretend that the truth was anything else, describing the little V-8 as an engine "big enough to move the Monza with effortless ease, yet small enough to let its two-barrel carburetor sip fuel sparingly—the way a small car engine should."

At mid-year, Chevrolet obliged would-be Monza owners who wanted more power by adding the L65 350 cid V-8 to the Monza's engine lineup. With 125 hp, it moved the 2+2 from zero to sixty miles per hour in less than 10 seconds, a substantial improvement over the thirteen second time of the 262 cid V-8 Monza. The installation of a V-8 in an engine compartment originally intended for a compact Wankel caused a service problem that went undetected during the Monza's development. When an owner or a Chevrolet mechanic wanted to replace the Monza's sparkplugs, he discovered it was impossible to remove those closest to the firewall. The only way to complete the procedure, Chevrolet conceded, was to partially unbolt the engine from the chassis and lift it approximately one-half inch with a hydraulic jack.

At the same time the 350 cid V-8 became a Monza option, a new model, called the Monza Towne Coupe, joined the line. Although the two Monzas were mechanically identical, the 2+2 shared few body panels with its notchback cousin. Instead of the 2+2's soft urethane-skinned front end and dual rec-

1972 Chevelle SS 350 Two-Door Hardtop / Owners: Doug and Cindy Starks

161

1973 Vega GT Kammback Wa

tangular headlights, a step which the 2+2 pioneered on American production automobiles, the Towne Coupe was fitted with single circular headlamps and conventional grille and bumper arrangement. For the 1977 model year the 2+2's urethane front end became a Towne Coupe option. The Towne Coupe's 177.8 inch length was 1.5 inches shorter than the 2+2's, and was 68 pounds lighter due to its fixed rear seat. With its squared-off and vinyl-covered roof, the Towne Coupe provided rear seat occupants with 1.9 inches of additional headroom.

Like the 2+2 and its lower-priced "S" variant, also a mid-year offering, the Towne Coupe was equipped with front bucket seats and individual rear seats. While the 2+2's interior with its leather-like vinyl upholstery, four-spoke steering wheel, center console and standard special instrumentation (including a tachometer), was intended to enhance its sports-car-like personality, that of the Towne Coupe emphasized luxury. A patterned cloth upholstery package was available and special sound insulation contributed to its more discreet image.

The Vega's standard 78 hp, 2.3 liter four-cylinder engine powered the S version of the 2+2, but the trio of 2+2 engines were optional on the Towne Coupe. Although it was an extra-cost option for the Towne Coupe and S models, a four-speed gearbox was standard on the 2+2. Included in the mid-year package of Monza changes and options was the first modern five-speed manual transmission manufactured in the U.S.

The visual impact of the 1977 Monza 2+2 equipped with the Z02 Spyder Appearance package suggested performance with a front air dam, rear spoiler, black body highlights and a fanciful Black Widow hood decal. Under the Spyder's hood was a 140 hp 305 cid V-8 allowing it easily to exceed the new federally mandated speedometer limit of 80 miles per hour.

In the meantime, the rest of Chevrolet, like the entire auto industry, rode through the first half of the Seventies on a roller coaster whose course was dictated by labor troubles, government regulation and a looming energy crisis. The Chevelle continued in its familiar guise through 1972 and in 1973 was significantly restyled, with new energy absorbing bumpers designed to comply with the government's five mile-per-hour bumper regulations. It was the last year for the SS model; it was replaced in 1974 by the S-3.

Unlike Chevrolet's larger models, the Nova remained a good seller through this period. Over 330,000 cars were sold in 1973; the following year its sales crept close to the 565,000 unit level of the full-size Chevrolet. A hatchback coupe version was added in 1973 and a restyling for 1975 made it better looking than ever. Perhaps as a response to Ford's new Mercedes-inspired Granada, the elegant 1975 four-door Nova LN bore more than a passing resemblance to the BMW's 530i coupe; indeed, *Road & Track* called it "a European Chevy."

Chevrolet's full-size models suffered the strongest impact from the "era of limits." Sales peaked in 1972 at 1,010,749 units, but slumped to just over 400,-000 in 1975. In Caprice, Impala and Bel Air versions, it still remained America's favorite full-size car. To set the Caprice off from its Impala sibling it was equipped with its own Cadillac-type grille; the 1974 to 1976 versions featured huge rear quarter windows fitted to the sail panels. Nineteen seventy-five would be the last year for Chevrolet's full-size convertible; 5275 examples were sold with a list price of $5258.

The debate over the styling of the Monte Carlo became even more pronounced when it was restyled in 1973. Despite its new "baroque" lines, the Monte Carlo took *Motor Trend's* 1973 Car of the Year award. Stylist Dave

1973 Vega Hatchback Coupe / Owner: General Motors Corporation

1973 Corvette Convertible / Owner: William E. Buie

Holls considers the 1973 Monte Carlo "the most successful car ever made at General Motors. We never made more money on a car than [on] that one." Some of the earliest proposals for the 1973 car included small "opera windows." They attracted so much attention that Irv Rybicki had them commandeered for Cadillac's Eldorado. "I think he was right," says Holls. "Something like that should start from a Cadillac so the rub-off is from a premium car."

Chevrolet's performance cars, the Camaro and Corvette, continued to suffer the federally mandated indignities begun in the early Seventies. Bumper regulations dictated a new urethane front end on the 1973 Corvette; the 454 cid Mark IV was still available for the year and even *increased* slightly in horsepower for 1973. The following year, the urethane treatment was used on the rear of the car; it was also the final year for the 454. The Camaro, including the high-performance Z-28, remained popular in spite of the energy crisis. The 1972 Norwood plant strike, however, left dealers with no cars to sell. Said *Motor Trend* in February 1973: "The first time most of these would-be Camaro/Firebird customers walked out a new car showroom's front door, flinty-eyed Chevy and Pontiac dealers kissed them goodbye." The Z28 left the lineup in 1975 and 1976; its replacement was a new Rally Sport, a far cry from the Z28's of yore.

At mid-decade Chevrolet was on the cusp of great change. The oil crisis, its long gas lines and 55 mph speed limit had sent designers back to the boards with orders to cut down weight, size and displacement. While the post-crisis market would fluctuate as wildly as with the price of gasoline, GM, and Chevrolet in particular, had learned some important lessons. A new era was underway; Chevrolet would soon again be building a better way to see the USA.

1973 Nova SS Two-Door Coupe / Owner: Kenneth F. Johnson

CHAPTER NINE

CHEVROLET

CHALLENGE FROM ABROAD

Chevrolet Confronts a New Market

The balloons and stage shows that were an expected part of a new car introduction began to disappear in the mid-Seventies, a fading symbol of an expansive past that was no longer appropriate. This was a new age, a new beginning, best symbolized by Chevrolet's selection of Washington, DC as the site for the September 16, 1975 announcement of its decision to produce the Chevette. Once described by a corporate spokesman as GM's "turboprop in the small car market," the Chevette was the first manifestation of a new corporate philosophy at General Motors.

In 1973 the mileage average of all GM automobiles was 12 mpg, the industry's worst. "Our sales of large cars just stopped," GM Chairman Pete Estes said afterwards in the July 1976 issue of *Fortune*. "We couldn't even get people into our showrooms, and we were in deep trouble. It was an emergency as far as we were concerned, and we decided that we had to move fast, just like a war." The corporation's share of the market the following year was forty-two percent, GM's poorest postwar performance, with the exception of the strike year in 1970. But these unfortunate milestones had been preceded by the establishment in 1972 of an ad hoc group, the Energy Task Force, headed by GM treasurer David C. Collier. By March 1973 its members had reached three significant conclusions: 1. An energy problem existed in the United States, 2. The federal government did not have any plan in hand to deal with it and 3. The inevitable change imminent in the structure of the foreign energy market would have a profound impact upon the automobile industry. With the automobile market of the early Eighties clearly under debate, these conclusions formed the basis of General Motors' product planning for the next decade.

With the goal of the ETF in hand, GM began to make significant steps towards improving the fuel economy of its automobiles. But the inadequacy of the rate at which these changes were originally to occur was underscored by GM president Gerstenberg's comment of March 21, 1974: "This market is telling us a hell of a lot. . . . We foresaw some of it down the road, but not with the acceleration since last October." On the afternoon of December 24, 1973, however, the GM Board of Directors took its first hesitant steps towards putting Chevrolet more in tune with the times of authorizing work to begin on an American version of GM's T-car. Development of this world car, known as Project 909, had started in mid-1970 as a successor to Opel's aging Kadett model. Of conventional front engine/rear drive design, it eventually was produced as the Chevette in Brazil, the Opel Kadett in Germany, the Isuzu Gemini in Japan, the K-180 in Argentina, the Holden in Australia and the Vauxhall Chevette in England.

Gerstenberg promised that if the American consumer wanted more small cars, "we are going to break our butt to get them for him." While Chevrolet did have a number of small car projects in the pipelines, none of them could be ready by 1975. On the other hand, there was a good possibility that an Americanized version of the T-car could be at Chevrolet dealers as a 1976 model.

John Mowrey, chief engineer of the Chevette project, had previously worked with Isuzu in Japan on their version of the T-car. Reviewing the results of Mowrey's new assignment, *Car and Driver* observed in its October 1975 issue: "The nasty lessons of the Vega—with its vibrations, overheating, rustouts and generally

F. James McDonald

shabby workmanship—have not been lost on General Motors and a great effort appears to have been expended in behalf of the Chevette's reliability factor." Although the target date for the Chevette's introduction left little room for error, GM took no chances of the Chevette's sales career being destroyed by recalls or reliability problems. Virtually none of the Chevette's body panels were interchangeable with those of the other T-cars and its underbody was totally redesigned for better corrosion protection.

The Chevette's front suspension, with two inches more travel than other contemporary Chevrolets, was fitted with tapered coil springs. At the rear were coil springs and trailing arms arranged in a fashion similar to the Opel 1900's. Opel also supplied the design of the Chevette's four cylinder engine which, despite an iron block, weighed fifty-nine pounds less than the Vega's alloy block engine. Among its more prominent features were a belt driven overhead camshaft, crossflow porting, a new Rochester "Monojet" carburetor and, for the first time on an American car, an underhood diagnostic system. The basic Chevette 1400 cc engine developed 52 hp, but for an additional $51, a larger 1600 cc version with 60 hp was available. Although the Chevette was offered only in a two-door hatchback version, Chevrolet provided five variations, each with unique features and characteristics. The bargain basement Chevette was the $2899 Scooter with no rear seat and an austere interior with vinyl upholstery and rubber floor mats. The Scooter was available in only four exterior colors and its power team was limited to the 1400 cc engine with a four-speed manual transmission. A step up from the Scooter was the Chevette Coupe, a full four-seater with more exterior bright work, an upgraded interior and additional acoustical insulation.

The application of black accents on the side windows and bumpers plus a set of lower body stripes converted the Coupe into the Chevette "Sports Coupe." If buyers found none of these options appealing, then Chevrolet offered the Woody Coupe, with "the stylish look of a mini-Estate wagon." Its special features included wood-grain vinyl exterior trim, a sport steering wheel, bright window moldings, wheel trim rings plus a "deluxe" grille with bright accents.

The Chevette with the most exciting performance was the Rally Coupe, whose standard equipment included the 1.6 liter engine, a rear stabilizer bar, "sport" shifter and steering wheel plus a special instrumentation package that featured a tachometer and temperature gauge. Externally, the Rally Coupe was identified by "Rally 1.6" decals, black rocker panels and special wheel covers.

At the Chevette's press introduction, Robert Lund predicted that Chevrolet would "sell 275,000 Chevettes in 1976 with 135,000 to 150,000 conquest sales from the imports." Chevette sales started with a backlog of nearly 77,000 orders, but within months dealers had large inventories of Chevettes on hand as gasoline supplies returned to normal. By April 1976, Chevrolet had reduced its production schedule by nearly fifty percent. It would not be until 1979 that the market would shift back again towards small cars, a result of sharply rising OPEC oil prices, along with spot shortages resulting from the federal government's allocation policy. GM admitted: "This turnabout occurred much more rapidly than the industry's ability to change its products and plants in response to these new demands. . . . The foreign manufacturers," continued GM, "were in position to capitalize

1974 Camaro Z-28 Sport Coupe / Owner: Jim Murauskis

1974 Chevelle Laguna S-3 Sport Coupe / Owner: David L. Deaton

1974 Nova "Spirit of America" Two-Door Coupe / Owner: W. H. Heinrich

1974 Caprice Classic Two-Door Coupe / Owner: Oscar R. Rupe

on this rapid demand shift in 1979 because of their excessive stock levels in the U.S. at that time and because they had been building the smaller vehicles consistent with the demand of their home markets.'' The front-wheel-drive Citation came on line in April 1979 but the Chevette, which Chevrolet described as ''the forerunner of America's cars of tomorrow,'' was equally well positioned to move with the new market trend. In both 1978 and 1979 it would be the best-selling subcompact in the U.S. and in its 1980 annual report GM told its stockholders that ''the Chevrolet Chevette and Chevrolet Citation ended 1980 in a virtual tie as the best-selling cars in the U.S. either domestic or foreign.'' From 1976 through 1980, Chevette sales exceeded one million units and by the end of 1981 they had topped the 1.5 million mark.

It would be misleading, however, to credit the Chevette's sales success solely to its small size and good fuel economy. Unlike the Vega's recall-plagued career with its concomitant quality control problems, the Chevette earned a reputation for reliable, trouble-free operation and, thanks to a strong effort by Chevrolet engineers, a stubborn resistance to rust and corrosion. After an extended 24,000 mile test, *Car and Driver* reported in its December 1976 issue that the ''Chevette is the most trouble-free, slam-the-hood-and-forget-it . . . machine we've ever encountered.''

Throughout its production, Chevrolet successfully refined the Chevette's basic design. In 1977 the EPA rating of its 1600cc engine was improved to 31 mpg city/43 highway (up from 30/39) while the horsepower of both engines was raised, the 1400cc version was now rated at 57 hp; the 1600cc at 63 hp. The Scooter was now given a rear seat as part of its standard equipment, although it could be deleted for credit. The Woody model did not return for an encore. Its replacement was the Chevette Sandpiper, available in either Antique White or Cream Gold and identified by special exterior trim featuring a stylized interpretation of sandpipers running across its rear quarter panel.

Chevrolet dropped the 1400cc engine from the Chevette line the following year, offering instead the 63 hp 1600cc engine with all models. For an additional $55 a ''High Output'' L-4 engine with 68 hp was available. While the Scooter still remained the Chevette's price leader, a four-door sedan with a hatchback gave the Chevette additional sales appeal. Chevrolet stretched the Chevette's wheelbase three inches to create the sedan's 97.3 inch floor plan. As compared to the coupe version, the four-door model had 3.5 inches more rear leg room and an additional 1.5 cubic inches of cargo area. In line with the policy of their foreign competitors, all 1978 Chevettes (with the exception of the Scooter) had as standard equipment a long list of items previously offered as options, including swing-out rear windows (on coupes), AM radio, center console and white stripe tires.

Although its decade-old front-engine/rear-drive concept put the Chevette at a disadvantage with the forthcoming, more advanced Citation and Celebrity models, its popularity, buttressed by the addition of a diesel version, remained strong into 1982. In early 1982, for example, its weekly production usually exceeded that of all other American-built automobiles.

Even before the Yom Kippur war of 1973 and the ascent of crude oil as a tool of Arab foreign policy, plans were underway at General Motors to trim some of the bulk from its full-size passenger cars. An April 1972 decision of the Product Planning Committee was modest, however, calling for a weight reduction of just 400 pounds.

Work on early design concepts for the 1977 Chevrolet Impala and Caprice

1975 Cosworth Vega Hatchback Coupe / Owner: Dr. Robert A. Maloy

models began in the Chevrolet Advanced Design studio late in 1972. The conclusions of the October 1973 Collier report took GM a step further in reducing the size of its automobiles and the Arab Oil Embargo finalized the plan. As stylist Chuck Jordan recalls: "When the Oil Embargo hit and more stringent fuel economy goals were mandated, our design approach on the car was proved to be even more valid and timely."

"For the first time, the criteria of the past had to change," said Chevrolet studio one chief designer Don Lasky. "Our design judgements had to change. We had to come up with the most highly innovative car we have ever designed." The program was directed at GM's full-size B- and slightly larger C-bodies, the former best represented by Chevrolet's Impala and Caprice models. "It was a logical direction," added Lasky, "Our previous B-cars simply became too heavy."

General Motors focused first on scaling down its full-sized sedans because, said Pete Estes, "our business was family cars, so we had to start there. If we had started on the bottom, there would have been a gap for a year or so when the competitors could have moved in." The mandated upper-end weight limit for the 1977 B-cars was established at 3950 pounds, nearly 700 pounds less than the typical 1976 full-size GM car. Other objectives included a 5.5 inch reduction in wheelbase, 2.3 inches less front overhang and 4 inches less width.

The result for Chevrolet was a major engineering and styling triumph. Robert Lund expressed the view that with its new models, Chevrolet wasn't just in tune with the times: "As a matter of fact," he said, "we're leading the tune." A "giant step . . . the most innovative car we had ever designed . . . a turning point . . . a new design standard" were typical of the way Chevrolet's designers described the results of their efforts. But it was really GM Chairman Thomas Murphy who, two years earlier at the Chicago Auto Show, had charted the future course of GM in general and Chevrolet in particular. "Our objective," said Murphy, "is to offer motorists cars suited to an energy-short world; cars they can afford to buy and operate in a world ridden by inflation; cars large enough or small enough to meet their particular needs, not somebody else's, and cars that will still meet all the stringent standards for safety and clean air now in effect."

The arrival of the new Chevrolets was obviously a far cry from the flamboyant fanfare of the Sixties. Said Murphy: "This is no ordinary program. This is going to be GM's answer to the times and we intend that it will be the loudest and clearest answer the auto world has ever heard. We are talking about the most comprehensive, ambitious, far-reaching and costly program of its kind in the history of our industry."

Though the new Chevrolet did not possess the sophisticated front-drive characteristics of the forthcoming Citation, Cavalier and Celebrity models, it was an appropriate car for the times. Whereas its 1976 counterpart languished in the number three sales slot, the 1977 full-size Chevrolet passed by Oldsmobile's Cutlass to become the nation's best-selling automobile. With a car so saleable, Chevrolet dealers had few complaints. Many of them regarded the new model as one of the best Chevrolets in the division's history; a car free from recalls and far closer to the motoring realities of the late Seventies than its Chrysler and Ford counterparts. "The most jaded car critics," said *Car and Driver* in October 1976, "are in fact tripping over each other trying to be first to anoint this sedan the best full-sized Chevrolet ever made." Even after two years of production, *Motor Trend* (November 1978) could report that the Chevrolet Caprice was "the strongest runner in the best-car-for-the-money sweepstakes in America."

Thomas R. Zimmer, chief engineer for the 1977 Chevrolet project, described it as "the most sophisticated program of structural design undertaken by Chevrolet. Our people have probably become the most expert in the world in new design technologies." While the GM engineers had to reduce what is today regarded as unnecessary exterior size and weight, and make more efficient use of the space allocated for passengers and luggage, they were not free to cut all the ties with Chevrolet's heritage. "First, the uppermost among the engineering objectives," said Zimmer, "was to maintain the sense of value which people have come to expect from the traditional-size Chevrolet."

Although Finite Element Analysis (FEA) and plastic prototype modeling techniques had been used for several years in the automobile industry, the 1977 Chevrolet was the first American automobile that benefitted from being developed with these techniques. FEA, which was derived from the aerospace industry, made possible computer programming of blueprint drawings prior to the construction of the first, full-scale metal prototype. Using a ⅜ scale plastic model, engineers tested components far more efficiently than by older, more expensive and time-consuming all-metal, working prototype approaches. As engineers reduced the size and weight of particular components, other opportunities to save weight appeared. At times, this procedure netted small returns, but the final tally showed an impressive 661 pound improvement over the 1976 model. Design changes in brake and suspension components, for example, shaved off 100 pounds, while improved bumpers were lighter by 150 pounds.

With less weight, the new Chevrolet could use less horsepower while maintaining decent performance. The big 400 and 454 cid V-8s of earlier days were no longer offered but their bulk was hardly missed. The most powerful V-8 available for 1977 was a 350 cid unit with a four-barrel carburetor producing 170 net horsepower. It virtually matched the acceleration of the older model with the 400 cid V-8.

For the first time since 1973, Chevrolet's 250 cid six cylinder engine was available in its full-sized model. Its EPA mileage estimate of 22 mpg highway and 17 city along with a zero to 60 mph time of 15.1 seconds represented a reasonable compromise between fuel economy and adequate performance. Amidst the great emphasis on weight reduction and fuel economy, Chevrolet's consistent wonder bargain, the $36 F–41 suspension package option, remained alive and well. *Car and Driver* in October 1976 described the F–41 as a feature "that'll make you think your Chevy came from the Black Forest instead of Detroit."

Like their engineering counterparts, the Chevrolet's stylists had as their objective the creation of an automobile that was right for the time, possessed an appearance characterized by efficiency and advanced thinking and provided increased riding comfort, roominess and ease of entry and exit. Reflecting upon the turnabout in design that the new Chevrolet's appearance represented, Chuck Jordan declared: "The longer, wider and lower automobile philosophy of the 1950's and 1960's is gone for good and has been replaced with a new lean, efficient look of crispness, elegance and simplicity." William Mitchell, GM's vice-president in charge of styling, considered the new Chevrolet a prime example of the "sheer look," which he admitted was influenced by the appearance of some Pininfarina cars, including the Fiat 130 Coupe. "While we didn't copy it as such," said Mitchell, "it had a lot to do with influencing us."

But the new Chevrolet was far more than a mere mixture of styling themes. More importantly, said Jordan, its forward thrust appearance and strong, fender-high horizontal line "mirrored the crisp wall construction of current architecture, the lighter weight clothing and the weight-watching diet consciousness of the early 70's." With obvious pride, Jordan predicted that "we'll look back on the Seventies as an era of automotive styling at the cross-roads, and on the '77 Chevrolet as being as innovative from a design standpoint as the Chevrolet Camaro or Monte Carlo were when first introduced."

Though the introduction of the Chevrolet Citation on April 19, 1979 as the "first Chevy of the Eighties" reflected the importance of the 1972 energy task force report, its corporate roots went considerably deeper. Two years before the production of the Vega began, Chevrolet research concluded that the market for small cars in the U.S. would undergo steady growth. While this forecast gained more and more adherents both in and out of GM, a special advanced design program headed by Claire MacKichan proposed a new front-wheel-drive small car as the Vega's eventual successor. Since, says Design Staff member Dick Ruzzin, one of the primary goals of the project was to design an efficient small family car, the front-wheel-drive package was strongly endorsed by MacKichan's team. During this program's early stages the Opel Ascona served as a benchmark design. "The Ascona," says Ruzzin, "had a very good conventional rear-wheel-drive package and the only way to improve upon this arrangement was by going to front-wheel-drive. We were able to envision a smaller, lighter car that had more interior room than the Opel."

Thus in early 1974 when Chevrolet general manager F. James McDonald assigned a group of his top designers, engineers and marketing staff members the task of determining the characteristics of the small family car of the future, they were by no means ignorant of the brave new automotive world.

There was also a general acknowledgement that Chevrolet's existing products would not be appropriate in the new energy environment. "We clearly did not have the vehicles in 1973," recalls Bob Eaton, "that had long term viability. We were going to have to retool essentially all of our product line." The Small Car Strategy Group, notes Eaton, who was one of its original members, "was active on a full-time basis for a number of months and made a complete examination of the market below the rear-wheel-drive Chevelle." There was also a clarification of the various transportation needs in the segment of the market, a review of some examples of how those needs might be filled, as well as an estimate of the market size. Therefore, explains Eaton, General Motors had in hand an analysis of "the opportunities that might be available to someone who might have the right product." The result of this analysis was the conclusion that Chevrolet's biggest need was a new product in the small family car market.

The car would clearly have to be of a different scope than that of a typical new car project at GM. "Our design approach to the S.F.C. [Small Family Car] was a drastic departure from our typical design philosophy. . . . We tried an approach of efficiency. Our goal was to make the car as lean and trim as possible, at the same time giving optimium interior comfort and space. Reducing weight was a major consideration. Every part that went into the car was carefully studied in relation to weight reduction."

For a brief time consideration was given to the development of a Citation-sized automobile with rear-wheel-drive. But this idea, stresses Bob Eaton, was mentioned "only in passing." Perhaps if Chevrolet already had "on the shelf" components to produce a car with the desired size and fuel consumption the debate between front- and rear-wheel-drive would have been more spirited. As Eaton

1975 Monza "S" 2 + 2 Hatchback Coupe / Owner: General Motors Corporation

points out, however, "If you don't have them, then there are clearly added advantages and efficiencies in a front-wheel design. You end up not considering to do it in any other way except for front-wheel-drive."

Although there were no specific limitations imposed upon the SFC staff, it was obvious that the SFC would be either equal to or superior in all major areas to the contemporary Nova and Monza models. Thus the SFC would provide room for five occupants, have more luggage space than the Monza, equal the Nova's performance with a smaller engine and be more economical than the Monza. In addition, the SFC was also to be available with the options popular with American consumers.

Regarding McDonald's original assignment, Lloyd Reuss, Chevrolet's director of product planning in 1974 and later Buick's general manager recalls: "The important thing, I think, with the assignment was not to take a look four years down the road, but to take a look at what we ought to have in the Eighties." Dick Ruzzin adds: "Maximizing driver visibility, control functions and general comfort were all major human factor considerations. Careful attention was placed upon the smallest detail. The resulting interior package was one of optimum driver compatibility." Reuss and the other members of the SFC program, which included Robert Eaton and Claire MacKichan with respective responsibilities for engineering and styling, were "broad horizon" people and while there was some initial disagreement about the direction the SFC program should follow, everyone, notes Reuss, "jumped in with both feet."

During the summer of 1974, the SFC team pored over the results of marketing research and dissected virtually every available front-wheel-drive automobile in production with, according to Eaton, an emphasis on imported front-wheel-drive cars. And the need for a new small Chevrolet to not only transport comfortably five people plus their luggage and provide good performance but also deliver from 25 to 35 percent better fuel mileage than a Nova became more and more apparent. Experiences with contemporary fuel efficient automobiles and a close liaison with Opel designers and engineers who were then also working on a new model led the SFC staff to conclude that nothing short of an all-new car, in the tracks of the 1969 Front Wheel Drive concept, and not just a rebodied or re-engineered version of an existing Chevrolet would be satisfactory.

The normal routine for Chevrolet's top engineers, designers and sales strategists included a monthly product planning meeting with general manager McDonald. Though meetings were seldom routine, the August meeting was even less so. "A lot of us," remembers Reuss, "didn't sleep the night before." The reason was that meeting's topic—the first formal report of the SFC project. "I remember quite distinctly," continues Reuss, "we made the presentation to McDonald in the Design Staff auditorium and as we walked outside to go over to the styling dome where we had the mockups, Jim said 'Gee, you're talking an all-new car from the ground up, you're not just talking about using anything.' And we said yes and his response to that was, 'Boy, I've got to think about this.' "

Bob Eaton recalls that the SFC group was dedicated to the philosophy encompassed by the study. "We all believed that if we could manage to get our points across, this project would turn out to be the future product plan for Chevrolet for years to come."

After the presentation McDonald returned to his office in the GM building in Detroit. Says Reuss: "He came back next morning and said, 'We've talked about this and you know, I'm really convinced that you've got something here and that this is probably the way we ought to be going.' "

While McDonald's enthusiasm for the SFC project didn't guarantee its eventual transformation into a production reality, it was headed in that direction and picking up momentum. The next crucial step was a gathering of most members of General Motors' executive committee and the general managers of the car and truck divisions for a "ride party" in February 1975 at the GM Phoenix, Arizona test grounds. On March 19, 1975 the corporation adopted the program as the next generation X-car or successor to the Nova-based GM compact. Though the last step was a clear go-ahead signal for the SFC to move to full production version status, momentum steadily picked up on the project and, according to Lloyd Reuss, "more and more people became convinced that this was in fact something we had to do as a corporation." The key catalyst remained McDonald who proceeded during 1975 to convince the corporation's officers that the multi-billion dollar SFC project was crucial to General Motors' future.

In December 1974 Robert Lund succeeded McDonald, who became executive vice president in charge of GM's Overseas Group, as Chevrolet's general manager. Lloyd Reuss remembers a plaque presented to McDonald before he left Chevrolet for his new position. "It had two crystal balls on it and on one was superimposed a likeness of the X-car. The other carried an impression of the Chevrolet S-Truck. The plaque was inscribed, 'Now that you're up and moving in the corporation, we hope that you will continue to see both of these products in the future.' "

The expansion of the SFC study from an exclusively Chevrolet program into a corporate-wide program took place in January 1976 when the project was released to the production studios of Pontiac, Oldsmobile, Buick and Chevrolet. This represented a turnabout on the part of some GM executives who, even after the February 1975 presentation, still felt that although the SFC was a good car for Chevrolet, it was not the type of vehicle that all divisions could market. "I remember a couple of guys then saying," recalls Reuss, "that it just wasn't the type of product for Buick and Oldsmobile." Reuss once felt that "a program this big and this radical, you don't sell in one shot." In spite of initial interest in the SFC program, Buick and Oldsmobile remained lukewarm.

In 1975, at the beginning of its evolution, the SFC wasn't a single car, but one with several derivatives. Previously, says Dick Ruzzin, Oldsmobile and Buick "had to use a Chevrolet Nova body with only minimal front and rear end panel changes. This new car offered them an opportunity to develop a car that was all Oldsmobile or Buick." The GM Design Staff proposed to achieve this by maintaining a high degree of interchangeable exterior sheet metal panels for the Chevrolet/Pontiac versions and "specific interchangeability" between Oldsmobile and Buick. Thus Chevrolet and Pontiac shared the five-passenger hatchback version; Buick and Oldsmobile the notchback sedan. Chevrolet had exclusive use of the semi-fastback coupe and the roof of the Pontiac two-door coupe was derived from the Oldsmobile/Buick version. This high degree of structural compatibility enabled General Motors, says Ruzzin, to "change from a coupe to a sedan by merely changing the doors and pillars. We had never successfully accomplished this before, and it meant a considerable saving in tooling costs for General Motors." In addition, there's little doubt that Reuss' new post as Buick's chief engineer in the fall of 1975 didn't hurt the prospects for a Buick X-car.

Chevrolet was the only GM division to develop a new name for its version of the X-car. Bob Lund, then general manager of the division, felt strongly that the

1975 Caprice Classic Convertible / Owner: W. H. Heinrich

1975 Corvette Convertible / Owner: Bob Brewer

car should have a new name, even though the Nova name was successful. Because the front-wheel-drive X-cars were such a radical departure for GM, Lund, says Ruzzin, "thought it was appropriate to identify the car with a new name." Thus though the Phoenix, Omega and Skylark titles were carried over from the older rear-wheel-drive models, the new front-wheel-drive Chevrolet came into the automotive world as the Citation.

The X-car was not the first automobile whose development was based upon the Project Center Concept, which *Fortune* regarded as "GM's single most important managerial tool in carrying out that bold decision to downsize." However, its magnitude dwarfed previous new car developments. "The time frame is important," says Reuss. "The way the new products came around in those days was when you reskinned old ones or put new bodies on them. You didn't tool up all-new engines, transmissions and axles." Robert Eaton, who was the manger of the X-car project, noted that the X-car "set up a structural program that was by far the largest ever undertaken by GM. In the process, we produced significant advances in the state of the art in this area." Nonetheless, Eaton also cites some advantage in the X-car's genesis as an exclusively Chevrolet project: "The program progressed for approximately one year before there was additional car division involvement and that really helped significantly because this was enough of a departure from anything we had previously done that, had we had total involvement, it might have been a little more difficult getting it off and going."

Half-scale models crashed into half-scale barriers yielded the same data as conventional, full-size crash testing but with a significant savings in time and expense. Likewise, FEA and CAD allowed a design to be thoroughly tested before it was built. Yet the costs for these advanced engineering methods remained staggering.

The X-body project center was established at GM's Technical Center in Warren, Michigan, but each division was assigned specific responsibilities. Using a Unified Project Code, the components of the future X-cars were divided into eleven separate categories. Chevrolet was responsible for development of the all-new V-6 engine and the cradle design for both this engine and the Pontiac in-line four. Pontiac also contributed the X-car's rear suspension, Buick prepared its brakes, transmission and exhaust system and Oldsmobile provided its steering system.

By April 1976, the first of five prototypes built at a cost of $650,000 per unit was operational and eventually 341 test vehicles were built and tested for 4,000,000 kilometers. In the early stages of the SFC project, quarter-scale models complete with engine, front and rear suspension and exhaust system were used to evaluate the car's aerodynamics. This was the first time such a technique had been used at GM and eventually two separate scale model tests were conducted, one at Cal Tech in Pasadena and the other at the Harrison wind tunnel at the GM Technical Center. In early 1975 a full-size model created by GM's Advanced Engineering was shipped to the Lockheed wind tunnel in Atlanta for additional aerodynamic fine tuning. As a result, notes Dick Ruzzin, "changes were made on the body surfaces to significantly reduce the drag coefficient." This effort, which eclipsed all previous aerodynamic projects by American automobile manufacturers, proved highly successful. The X-car's drag coefficient of 0.417 (the Nova's was 0.497) made it the slipperiest of all Chevrolets, except for the Camaro. Said Norm Sholler, chief body engineer for the X-body, "it requires less road force than the Chevette to keep it rolling at 50 mph." Yet the X-car had almost thirty percent more passenger and luggage space than Chevrolet's sub-compact Monza.

1976 Chevette Woody Two-Door Coupe / Owner: Malcolm D. Camuso

Although Chevrolet's Impala/Caprice and Malibu models had earlier been downsized to improve their fuel efficiency, many of their principal components had been of pre-1973 design. But, said Norm Sholler, "the Citation was designed from scratch. We had a chance to design fuel economy into almost every part." Although the most important single contributor to the Citation's fuel economy advantage over the Nova was its size and weight reduction, Sholler noted that "by gaining a trifle here and a trifle there, we were able to more than double the improvement attributable to weight reduction alone." An extensive computer analysis provided some theoretical improvements in fuel economy: mass reduction, 3.8 mpg; 24% less aerodynamic drag, 1.2 mpg; 15% less tire rolling resistance, 0.7 mpg; reduced front disc brake drag 0.3 mpg.

When the Citation debuted on April 19, 1979, comparisons were quickly made with the Nova and other Chevrolet models. On virtually every standpoint it eclipsed the old Nova models, though the Citation's passenger accommodations were compatible with those of the larger Malibu and Impala/Caprice. The Citation was, for example, 20 inches shorter, nearly 4 inches narrower and 800 pounds lighter than a two-door Nova coupe, yet it possessed 0.3 inches more front seat headroom, just a half-inch less rear seat headroom and came within an inch of matching the Malibu in virtually every other measurement of passenger accommodation. Its luggage capacity, at 20.1 cubic feet, was just 0.1 cubic feet less than the Impala's.

The most popular member of the Citation lineup was powered by the 151 cid four-cylinder 90 bhp engine coupled with the optional three-speed automatic transmission. The most sensational Citation was equipped with RPO B4X, more commonly known as the X-11 option. Chevrolet touted the X-11 as "the first performance model of the '80's" and though it did not quite rival the high-performance Chevrolet musclecars of the past, it blended the Citation's fuel efficient design with respectable performance. The 115 bhp V-6 (an option on any Citation) and a four-speed manual gearbox gave the X-11 a 0-60 mph time in the ten-second range. Rapid acceleration was not the new decade's sole measurement of performance, however; equally important were handling and road worthiness, areas in which the standard Citation excelled and the X-11 version proved sensational. MacPherson struts were used for the Citation's coil spring front suspension. Its rear suspension also utilized coil springs with a lightweight trailing arm

1976 Caprice Classic Four-Door Sedan / Owner: Ed Martin

and a built-in stabilizer bar.

Although many elements of the X-11 package (which was available only on the two-door notchback and hatchback Citations) were appearance enhancement items such as a black-out paint scheme, X-11 insignia, a rear spoiler, dual sport mirrors, the F41 suspension package, was available on any Citation for just $27 and continued to be one of Detroit's best performance bargains. Its stiffer springs, shocks, larger front and rear stabilizer bars plus P205/70R steel belted radial tires gave the X-11 taut road manners that made believers out of Detroit's most cynical critics. Its 63 mph exit speed after traversing *Road & Track's* demanding 700 ft. slalom test was inferior to only two other cars tested by the magazine, the Corvette and the Lamborghini Countach. Among the cars that the X-11 outperformed were the Mercedes-Benz 450 SEL, BMW 633 CSi and Mazda RX-7. Seldom had *R&T* been so impressed by an American car. "The X-11," it reported, "is equally at home on any twisty road . . . we have little trouble stating it is probably the best car ever from Detroit, and one of the best regardless of country of origin or manufacturer."

The Citation quickly became the best selling new car Chevrolet had ever introduced, an impressive achievement considering the depth and breadth of Chevrolet history. With Citation sales in the first month totalling 31,602, Chevrolet general manager Robert D. Lund was confident that Chevrolet's extensive development work had paid off. "Citation is proving to be the right car at the right time." Indeed it was. The Citation's strong sales pace, with over 180,000 sold in the first six months of production, enabled it to establish the best first-year sales record of any new car ever produced by General Motors. "Never in our history," said Lund, "has a new car been so well received. Never has one sold so well, been in such demand and continued to generate such excitement throughout the Chevrolet organization."

Changes in the Citation for 1981 were minor: a new grille design, a new floor-mounted automobile gearshift for use with an optional center console, an optional reclining backrest for the driver's seat and the availability of front bucket seats in combination with the Citation's standard interior. The slow-selling two-door notchback sedan was dropped from the Citation lineup. As before, the X-11 option included its own unique appearance package and instrumentation. The F41 suspension option continued to be available on all Citations, but when installed on the X-11 model in included P215/60R steel belted radial tires. Also new on the 1981 X-11 was a 135 hp, H0660 (High Output, 6 cylinder, 60 degrees) engine (also available for use in any model as option LH7) that powered the Citation to a new level of performance excellence. The X-11, said *Motor Trend,* was "the snappiest, sexiest thing offered by any American manufacturer for 1981."

Chevrolet further fine-tuned the Citation for 1982. The standard 2.5 liter four received throttle-body electronic fuel injection which boosted its fuel economy. With the standard four-speed manual transmission, EPA mileage estimates were 26 mpg city and 41 mpg highway, up from 22 and 35 respectively in 1981. Other mechanical changes included high pressure 35 psi tires, relocated rack and pinion steering and a two degree positive camber adjustment to the front suspension.

The limpid automobile market of 1982 prompted Chevrolet to reintroduce the two-door "slant back" Citation coupe model in January 1982. Its retail price of $6297.27 was $457 under the price of the hatchbacks. "This new Citation Coupe," said Robert Lund, "should signal Chevrolet dealers and customers alike of our aggressive response to the marketplace—to satisfy the needs of the times." 179

CHAPTER TEN

CHEVROLET TODAY AND TOMORROW

A New Technology for the Future

Few automobiles in Chevrolet history were more carefully conceived than the Cavalier, known more commonly in GM's lexicon as the J-car. Even fewer were so eagerly awaited and perhaps none, other than the Corvair, were off to a stormier start. At its introduction in May 1981, Chevrolet general manager Lund proclaimed that the Cavalier was "going to battle against the best equipped cars—both domestic and foreign—in the most competitive time period in recent automobile history. It's a battle we aim to win." There were many, even among Chevrolet's competitors, who hoped Lund's prediction was correct. After thirty long months of depressed sales, consistently high interest rates and faltering rebate programs, the industry was desperately looking for a car whose fresh appeal would lead it out of the sales doldrums.

The design mandates for the Cavalier were stringent. "We told the designers," recalled Lund, "we wanted well-equipped cars with room for four people to ride in comfort. We wanted optimum space utilization, optimum aerodynamics and optimum performance, ride and handling. And of course we wanted the best appearing car in the market—the best fits and finishes. It was a very complex and challenging exercise."

Surveys of both dealers and potential customers led to the decision to offer the Cavalier with a long list of features as standard equipment. Over seven hundred individuals (50 percent male, 50 percent under age 35 and 50 percent intending to purchase a foreign car) were queried by Chevrolet's marketing staff in product clinics held in Houston and Atlanta during 1979.

Although the J-car platform was to be shared by all GM divisions, Chevrolet was responsible for the bulk of its development, including the engine, manual transaxle and front suspension, and it made extensive use of lessons learned in downsizing the Impala/Caprice and in the creation of the Citation. Thus the Cavalier was the beneficiary of sophisticated FEA techniques and, in its assembly, automatic robot-controlled laser optic inspection. Aerodynamic studies at the Lockheed Marietta wind tunnel gave the Cavalier impressive drag coefficients of 0.396 for the hatchback and 0.45 for the station wagon.

The Cavalier's 88 horsepower 1.8 liter four, state-of-the-art front-drive layout, lengthy list of standard equipment and its choice of coupe, sedan or station wagon body styles seemed to give it a strong competitive position with which to face the opposition from Japan. And its 101-inch wheelbase offered the exterior dimensions of a subcompact but the interior room of a compact.

Still, Cavalier sales failed at first to live up to the car's promise. One problem was Chevrolet's understandable concern about quality. Said chief engineer Roger Masch: "The customer's initial impression of a vehicle's fit and finish greatly affects his opinion of its potential need for service. Cavalier's coachwork quality is outstanding—maybe the best in Chevrolet history." But this insistence on quality resulted in a supply of only six thousand units in dealers' hands during the crucial launch period.

A second setback to the Cavalier's early sales took the form of a new phenomenon known as "sticker shock." Buyers found it difficult to accept the Cavalier's technological advances—and long list of standard equipment—when they were accompanied by a base price of almost $7000, substantially more than a Citation,

Robert D. Lund

Robert C. Stempel

Robert D. Burger

or even a full-size Impala. The American car market was falling apart in the summer of 1981 and even after production picked up, sales did not follow. In October 1981, for example, Cavalier sales numbered just 14,398.

Compounding the problem were complaints about the Cavalier's performance and handling. "Viewed in the hard light of mid-1981 market," wrote automotive iconoclast Brock Yates in *The Decline and Fall of the American Automobile Industry*, "the J-cars were little more than modest counterfeits of machinery the Japanese were beginning to phase out and replace." It was not an auspicious beginning for a car that was intended to bring disenchanted Americans back to domestically-built automobiles.

Still reeling from the Cavalier's rebuff by the changed small car market of the Eighties, Chevrolet introduced the Celebrity, its new A-body car slated eventually to replace the Malibu. Behind the Citation and Cavalier, it was the third entry in GM's multi-billion dollar front-drive development program. Sharing several newly developed components with the revised 1982 Citation, the Celebrity was created as a fuel efficient front-wheel-drive family sedan, already far in advance of the old Malibu. At its introduction, it was offered with three different powerplants: Pontiac's 2.5 liter ohv four, a 2.8 liter Chevrolet-built V-6 and a brand-new 4.3 liter Oldsmobile V-6 diesel.

The Celebrity's $8300 base price included a long list of standard equipment, such as automatic transaxle, power brakes and steering, front and rear stabilizer bars, bodyside moldings and fiberglass-belted radial tires. Extensive aerodynamic testing, combined with flush-mounted window glass, integrated rear-view mirrors and rear deck spoiler made it possible for the Celebrity to slice through the wind at a steady 50 mph using only 11.5 horsepower, just slightly more than the Cavalier and substantially less than the Citation.

But as unemployment moved past the nine percent mark and interest rates remained stubbornly high, Chevrolet couldn't shake off a sales decline that saw its portion of General Motors sales shrink from nearly 49 percent in 1975 to 38 percent by the end of 1981.

Starting on February 1, 1982, the man who had to deal with this grim but certainly reversible reality was general manager Robert C. Stempel. His career at GM began in 1958 at Oldsmobile where he eventually became assistant chief engineer. By October 1974 he was Chevrolet's chief engineer in charge of engines and components, from which he was promoted to director of Chevrolet engineering in October 1975. Three years later he became general manager at Pontiac and prior to his return to Chevrolet, Stempel was managing director of Opel.

While economic conditions in Europe were anything but tranquil, those awaiting Stempel's return to Detroit were nothing short of horrendous. With interest rates soaring, consumer confidence at an all-time low and twenty-eight percent of new car sales captured by imports, the U.S. auto industry had plunged into its worst sales slump in over two decades. For the first time, annual automobile sales in Europe exceeded those in the U.S., and while the American automobile industry had thirty percent more capacity than needed to meet current demand, the Japanese had increased their capacity by thirty percent since 1978. No longer did the American automobile industry hold sway; in 1980 Japanese auto manufacturers

1977 Camaro Rally Sport LT Two-Door Coupe / Owner: Richard Carlton Cupp

outproduced the Americans 11,042,844 to 7,870,213. And no longer, it appeared, could a Chevrolet general manager anticipate his products controlling nearly a third of the marketplace. Said Stempel: "My own personal goal is to get back to twenty percent. I think the days of Chevrolet having thirty percent of the cars are just not there from the standpoint that there are too many competitors. And there are too many *good* competitors. They are not going to go away."

But amidst the gloom and doom prevalent in Detroit in 1982, Stempel noted several bright spots peeking over the automotive horizon. Chevrolet's S-10 light truck (which Stempel regarded as having quality second to none in its field) quickly found a willing audience, putting an end to the Japanese dominance of this market. Just as successful was the third generation Camaro. Work had begun in the summer of 1978 on a replacement for the Camaro model introduced in 1970. The first priority was the reestablishment of the performance standard for the Z28 from which all attributes of the other Camaro versions would derive.

Few American cars have been so dramatically styled as the 1982 Camaro. Based on an original theme by Roger Hughet and refined in Chevrolet Studio Three under the direction of Jerry Palmer, the new Camaro was more than a worthy successor to the second generation design (which had endured since 1970). It was, without qualifications, one of the best American design efforts of all time.

Within six months the Camaro was Chevrolet's hottest-selling car, and in Z28 form, the recipient of the *Motor Trend* Car of the Year award and the pace car for the 1982 Indianapolis 500. This latter honor prompted the production of 6360 replicas of the Indy pace car marketed as "Commemorative Editions."

By any standard and certainly true in the fast-paced environment of the Eighties, the Monte Carlo appeared to be an "old car." In 1978 its third generation form—downsized and lighter than the 1973-77 models—had debuted to model year sales of over 350,000 units. That level couldn't be maintained, however, and the Monte Carlo's popularity began to fade. The first "aerodynamic" Monte Carlo was introduced in 1981, with wind-tunnel tested sheet metal and a 10 percent reduction in drag from the 1980 model's level. But sales slid steadily downward to the 1982 model year, when just 105,721 were sold.

Despite its lackluster success in the showroom, the Monte was a resounding success at the speedways. To further reduce aerodynamic drag, and to aid high-speed stability, Chevrolet debuted the slope-nosed and bespoilered Monte Carlo SS in 1983. Raced by drivers such as Bobby Allison, Cale Yarlborough and A.J. Foyt, it dominated competition for the NASCAR Winston Cup Manufacturer's Championship that year. The street SS (officially an option package adding $1283 to the price tag) was powered by a new 5.0 liter 175 hp V-8. The only transmission offered was Turbo-Hydramatic with a higher-than-stock stall speed, crisper shifting and improved cooling. Backing up the engine was a full F41 sport suspension, with front and rear sway bars and P215/65R15 Goodyear Eagle GT's on 15x7-inch wheels—the largest ever mounted on a Monte Carlo.

At the other end of the spectrum, Cavalier sales received a major boost in September, 1982 when the Cavalier began its second model year with a larger displacement, 2.0 liter engine and electronic fuel injection, providing 10 percent more torque. A five-speed transmission was offered as an option. A new addition to the lineup came from a look backward rather than forward. During 1982 Chevrolet had sent a prototype Cavalier convertible out on the show circuit. The result was the mid-1983 introduction of a soft-top Cavalier, the first 500 of which were fitted with a white exterior and blue upholstery. They quickly fulfilled Stem-

pel's prediction that "we're sure it will create a lot of excitement and increase showroom traffic." Whereas sales in calendar years 1981 and 1982 had been 78,540 and 121,392 respectively, those for 1983 reached 259,397 cars, a level exceeded only by Ford's Escort and the Oldsmobile Cutlass Supreme.

Almost as successful as the Cavalier was the evergreen Chevette, of which over 2.4 million had been sold by late 1985. As late as the mid-Eighties, over ninety percent of all Chevettes built were still in use. In 1979 and again in 1981, the Chevette was Chevrolet's best-selling car.

But while the Chevette remained a successful seller, Stempel was realistic about its long-term appeal. Chevrolet's success, he realized, rode on its ability to offer it customers entry-level cars that could compete with foreign products in both price and value. His outlook for the future was pragmatic: "The current boss," he said of himself, "doesn't like high-priced Chevrolets—the current boss is interested in selling cars at an affordable price." He was determined to produce an automobile with fit, finish and longevity that would satisfy the most fastidious customer. Yet his initial goals were modest: he wanted to get people into Chevrolet showrooms to see how Chevrolet had changed, and in the process move Chevrolet's market share from 16.2 percent in 1982 to 16.6 percent in 1983.

But it was not to be. Although GM reported record profits of $4.2 billion for 1983, a healthy change from 1980's dismal loss of $763 million, the balance sheet masked problems in the company's lower-priced car lines. And that meant Chevrolet. Chevy's market share in 1978 had been 20.8 percent; by 1983 it had fallen to 14.8 percent. Compounding problems for GM in general and Chevrolet in particular were consumer complaints about X-car brakes. The NHTSA received its first complaint about locking rear brakes in July 1979; two years later, the agency had recorded a total of 212 complaints involving fifty-eight accidents and fourteen injuries. An initial recall of 47,000 vehicles failed to resolve the problem to NHTSA's satisfaction, and by 1983 an official finding by NHTSA of defective rear brake design prompted GM to recall 240,000 X-cars for brake repairs. Doubts about its safety took a substantial toll on Citation sales, which fell from 378,000 in 1980 to 210,000 in 1982. The combined effects of these problems took a substantial toll on the division's morale as well. Said one industry observer: "Chevrolet lost a pile of money last year [1983] despite a good year overall, and the company is stuck with a lot of small cars that don't work."

With so dismal a backdrop, it was not surprising that the new year brought word of tremendous changes at GM—changes that would particularly affect Chevrolet. On Monday, January 2, 1984, GM chairman Roger Smith announced the most sweeping reorganization in the corporation's history. GM's five car divisions and its Canadian car operations were reorganized into two groups, each of which would take total responsibility for the cars it produced. The GM Assembly Division and Fisher Body Division were disbanded and their functions handed over to the two new groups, Buick-Oldsmobile-Cadillac (BOC) and Chevrolet-Pontiac-GM of Canada (CPC). The intended result of this shakeup was to increase the decision making power of staff at every level and to loosen chains of command. The individual divisions were retained as marketing arms, but the reorganization was intended to streamline the amount of time needed to bring a car from concept to creation.

Heading the two divisions were Lloyd Reuss (CPC) and Bob Stempel (BOC). The new opening in Chevrolet's management was filled by Robert D. Burger, whose career with GM had started with Fisher Body in 1942. After twenty-four 183

1977 Monza Mirage Two-Door Hatchback Coupe / Owner: Lange and Runkel Chevrolet

1977 Impala Four-Door Sedan / Owner: Brenda Spears

1978 Malibu Classic Two-Door Coupe / Owner: Chevrolet Motor Division

1979 Nova Four-Door Sedan / Owners: Joseph and Linda Ehrhart

185

years at Oldsmobile, Burger was elected vice president of the GM sales and marketing staff in 1977 and became general manager of Cadillac in 1982.

Along with a new leader, other changes began to emerge fast and furious at Chevrolet. Since 1980, GM had been seriously assessing its ability to manufacture competitively priced small cars in the U.S. At the time, it was thought that only Japan could compete with Japan; and now a decision had been reached that would make Chevrolet GM's small car division. Chevrolet responded with a three-pronged assault on the hotly-contested small car market, beginning with the purchase of small cars made by Japanese firms and sold in the U.S. under the Chevrolet nameplate and culminating in the actual manufacture in the U.S. of a Japanese automobile.

Chevrolet received its first proposal for a Japanese-built subcompact from Isuzu in early 1981. Isuzu was hardly an unknown quantity at GM, since the corporation owned 34.3 percent of Isuzu's stock at the time. Isuzu was also a familiar name within Chevrolet, having already built the successful "LUV" compact pickup. The R-car, as the Isuzu project was called, was originally conceived as a Holden product, but gradually emerged as the ideal front-drive successor to the Chevette. "Our needs," said Tom McDaniel, a member of GM's Worldwide Planning Group who later became Chevrolet's director of international programs, "fit very nicely into what they wanted to do."

Meanwhile, Suzuki, better known in the U.S. for two-wheeled products, was looking for a U.S. partner to sponsor the M-car, a forthcoming 1.0 liter "sub-mini." Suzuki wanted the help of a partner experienced in the development of products for the North American market. Through Isuzu, Chevrolet learned of Suzuki's interest in marketing the car in the U.S. and GM responded in August of 1981 by buying a 5.3 percent stake in the company and committing to substantial technical assistance in the creation of a U.S. version of the M-car.

Although Chevrolet's original plans had called for only a single car, the complementary combination of Sprint and Spectrum led to Chevrolet's commitment to both cars, creating what McDaniel called "a win-win situation for us." Both projects were approved by GM in October, 1981.

The first of the two to appear in Chevrolet showrooms was the M-car, which would be called the Sprint when wearing a bowtie emblem. At its introduction on June 1, 1984, it was at once the smallest car ever sold by an American manufacturer and the largest ever made by Suzuki. Initially, distribution was limited to nine west coast states, but sales were brisk, thanks to the little car's under-$5000 base price. Despite its modest pricetag, the Sprint was technically competitive with far larger cars. Its three-cylinder, 1.0 liter, overhead-cam engine weighed just 147 pounds, but was capable of "sprinting" to 60 mph in just 13 seconds. Although its wheelbase measured just 88 inches and its overall length 141, the Sprint offered room for four. Not surprisingly, this compact package delivered excellent fuel economy, hitting the top of the EPA charts with ratings of 44 mpg/city and 50 mpg/highway.

When asked why Chevrolet didn't build the Sprint in the U.S., McDaniel didn't mince words. "We could not build this car in the United States and sell it for the low price we need to successfully market Sprint. GM did a detailed study on a small car in 1980-81 . . . the so-called 'S-car.' It would have been introduced as a 1984 model [as a successor to the Chevette] except for one thing. The cost study showed that Japanese manufacturers could build a comparable vehicle for at least $1500 less in Japan than could General Motors in the United States."

1979 Monte Carlo Two-Door Coupe / Owner: Dick Masheter Ford, Inc.

Larger than the Sprint, the Isuzu-built Spectrum was available in two and four-door models with prices of $6295 and $6575 respectively when it was introduced in the fall of 1984 in sixteen east coast states. Also front-wheel drive, the Spectrum was powered by an all-new 1.5 liter four producing 70 horsepower and capable of 38 mpg city and 43 highway.

The third step of this complex process was perhaps the most controversial. On February 17, 1983 General Motors joined as an equal partner with Toyota to form New United Motor Manufacturing, Inc. (NUMMI). As a joint venture, NUMMI was designed to combine the best talents of each company to produce a derivative of the Toyota Corolla at a former GM plant in Fremont, California. In December of 1984, less than twenty-two months after the signing of the agreement, the first Novas rolled off the assembly line.

Although these new models would not enter the overall sales picture until late 1984 or early 1985, Chevrolet's 1984 model year was shaping up just fine. The Cavalier was at last finding its stride. As it entered its fourth year with only modest changes, the Cavalier became, in terms of both 1984 calendar year sales

1980 Caprice Classic Two-Door Coupe / Owner: General Motors Corporation

1981 Monte Carlo Landau Two-Door Coupe / Owner: Center Chevrolet

1981 Chevette Four-Door Hatchback Sedan / Owner: Bob McDorman Chevrolet

1982 Chevrolet Citation Four-Door Hatchback Sedan / Owner: Dan Young Chevrolet

1982 Cavalier Type 10 Two-Door Hatchback Coupe / Owner: Dan Young Chevrolet

(377,545) and production (400,254), America's most popular automobile.

Nearly as attractive to the automotive public was the Celebrity, whose numbers were augmented with the addition of a station wagon model in 1984, helping to make it the most popular intermediate-size car for 1984 with model year sales of 307,777. Mixed in with this multitude was the new Celebrity Eurosport. Unlike Pontiac, which elected to offer its customers the fully equipped 6000STE sport sedan, Chevrolet chose to market a Eurosport trim and suspension (F11) package modestly priced at $199 and allow customers to pick and choose their way across the option sheet to their heart's content.

Performance was fast resuming its traditional role throughout the Chevrolet lineup. By 1985, when Darrell Waltrip won the NASCAR National Championship with a Monte Carlo, the problems of stability at 200-plus mph forced Chevrolet to again re-think the aerodynamics of the old mid-size coupe. The result was the 1986½ Monte Carlo SS Aerocoupe. With a sloping rear backlight reducing rear lift, the latest SS model sported a drag coefficient of 0.365, down from the 0.375

figure of the notchback version. Only 100 Aerocoupes were built in 1986, each priced at $13,751.

Thanks to the renewed American interest in performance, spurred by falling gas prices, the Camaro continued to ride the crest of a steady flow of technical refinements, foremost among them the introduction of the IROC-Z in 1985. The International Race of Champions (IROC) originated in 1973 as a series in which a select group of the world's best race car drivers competed in identical cars. After a three-year hiatus, the series resumed in 1984 with Cale Yarborough emerging the winner. With the exception of the first year, when the Porsche Carrera RSR was the car of choice, all IROC series have been campaigned with Camaros.

The IROC racing Camaros were styled in Chevrolet Studio Three and although they debuted prior to the production version, they were closely related to the 1985 Z28 and IROC-Z street Camaros. Not surprisingly, the IROC-Z became the top Camaro model. Although it shared the Z28's front fascia, a lower air dam and peripheral "ground effects" body skirting, the IROC-Z was visually set apart by

1982 Camaro Z-28 Two-Door Sport Coupe / Owner: Chevrolet Motor Division

its grille-mounted fog lamps, graphics and single-color paint scheme.

Designer Jerry Palmer liked to call the Camaro a "wheel-oriented" car and the IROC-Z was not short-changed in this category with 16x8-inch aluminum-alloy wheels and unidirectional Goodyear 245/50VR16 Gatorback tires. Its suspension included gas-filled Bilstein shocks in the rear, a 24 mm sway bar (shared with the Z28), an increase in caster from three to four degrees and increased effort power steering. In addition, a new crossmember was bolted in just below the front sway bar for a tighter structure and enhanced steering precision. Contributing to a lower center of gravity was a drop of 0.59 inches in overall height as compared to the Z28. The net result of these changes was a car capable of a lateral acceleration approaching 0.9 g.

Exclusive to the Z28 and IROC-Z was the LB9 5.0 liter V-8 fitted with electronic port fuel injection and a longer duration cam. With power outputs of 215 hp at 4400 rpm and torque of 275 lb/ft at 3200 rpm it was only available with a four-speed automatic. Proving Ground test results showed a 0-60 mph time of 7.1

seconds and a quarter-mile run time of 15.1 seconds.

Still poised at the top of Chevrolet's performance ladder was the Corvette. A new generation Corvette had emerged in 1984—only the second total redesign in Corvette history. The Corvette had retained its basic shape since 1968, and that shape was firmly rooted in the public's perception of the car. Once again, the task of updating a classic design landed on the shoulders of Jerry Palmer.

Looking back at what was the first totally new Corvette designed under his supervision, Palmer noted, "I really believe we've designed a car without compromise. But we've managed to retain a Corvette identity. It has a Corvette 'face' . . . . The first time that people see this car they're going to know what it is. They're going to say, 'Hey! That's a new Corvette!' "

Even with a $21,800 price, which placed the Corvette beyond the reach of many longtime Corvette fans (Chevrolet hoped the IROC-Z would fill the gap), the new model maintained a great Corvette tradition—offering a level of performance far beyond that of comparably priced cars. David McLellan, then serving as Corvette

1982 Chevrolet Celebrity CL Four-Door Sedan / Owner: Helen E. Spires

1983 S-10 Blazer / Owner: Chevrolet Motor Division

chief engineer, noted, "Even in base suspension configuration, the new Corvette is a sports car absolutely superior to any production vehicle in its part of the market. To find even a peer to this vehicle, you have to look at cars produced in extremely limited numbers and at prices traditionally two or three times that of the Corvette."

This wasn't to say that the Corvette was perfect; few cars start their production lives free from any shortcomings. During the 1984 model run numerous changes took place, among them provision for an overdrive lockout on the manual transmission and the inclusion of the 16-inch wheels from the Z51 handling package as standard equipment. A year later the Corvette's tendency to squeak and rattle its way across America was tamed, the instrumentation panel graphics were improved and the Delco-GM/Bose sound system was reworked.

Further changes took place in 1985 when the throttle-body fuel injection system was replaced by a tuned port version to create the 5.7 liter L98 V-8 with 230 hp (up from 205) at 4000 rpm and 330 lb/ft of torque (up from 290) at 2900 rpm. Whereas the 1984 model had a top speed above 140 mph, the 1985 version's upper limit exceeded 150 mph. All 1986 Corvettes were fitted with a computerized anti-lock braking system based on the Bosch ABS II system.

For anyone still mourning the demise of the Corvette convertible in 1975, or who simply felt the form of the latest model was a natural for an open version, 1986 was the year of deliverance. As the first Corvette convertible in over a decade, it became the seventh Chevrolet since 1948 to pace the Indianapolis 500. Needing no modifications for the race, all 1986 convertibles were virtual pace cars. With the arrival of the convertible, all Corvettes also received an engine with aluminum heads, allowing room for larger intake ports and providing a 9.5:1 compression ratio. Changes to the convertible's suspension included a slightly higher ride height to make room for the "K" brace used to stiffen the chassis.

Chevrolet, by 1985, was putting more and more effort into the promotion of mid-size, compact and subcompact cars which together comprised nearly eighty percent of the total passenger car market. Yet the automobile that had spurred the down-sizing movement back in 1977, the Impala/Caprice, remained just about everyone's favorite in the traditional family-size class. Although more aerodynamic sheet metal had replaced the original form in 1980, the Caprice's appearance

1984 Chevrolet Corvette Sport Coupe / Owner: Chevrolet Motor Division

1985 Astro Van / Owner: Chevrolet Motor Division

remained almost unchanged nearly a decade after its introduction. Moreover, sales continued to be healthy, never falling below the 200,000 mark and for 1984 reaching 258,902, which was only 2917 less than the 1980 level. For the 1985 calendar year sales were 245,826.

Throughout 1986 performance models continued to grow in popularity. The IROC-Z ended the year accounting for nearly 25 percent of Camaro Z28 sales. During the first five months of 1986 the Eurosport Celebrity represented almost one of every four Celebrity sales. With the Celebrity becoming the best-selling car in America during 1986, the Eurosport's popularity became even more significant.

Easing the already fading memories of the Cavalier's initially flat performance was the Z24 version for 1986, accurately promoted as a Sixties-style muscle car cast in the idiom of the Eighties. Flared rocker panels, a front air dam, special front and rear fascias, blacked-out trim, red badges, 14-inch rally wheels and Z24 identification added up to make a strong ''get going or get out of the way'' statement. Providing the go to match the show was the Z24's engine—Chevrolet's 2.8 liter V-6 with 120 hp at 4800 rpm and 155 lb/ft of torque at 3600 rpm.

Chevrolet's performance emphasis continued in the 1987 lineup. Both the Celebrity and Cavalier were offered with Chevrolet's second-generation 2.5 liter V-6 with 130 hp and a German-built Getrag five-speed manual transmission. The combination was standard for the Z24 Cavalier and optional throughout the Celebrity line. Among the V-6's technical highlights were an overall weight reduction of thirty-five pounds relative to the old 2.8 liter it replaced—thanks to new production techniques, redesigned cylinder heads, aluminum valve rocker arms and numerous other aluminum components.

The performance of the Sprint and Spectrum literally got a boost with the availability of turbocharged versions. The Sprint Turbo, available only as a two-door with a five-speed transmission, produced 70 hp and provided a 0-60 mph time of 9.5 seconds. The Spectrum Turbo came only as a four-door sedan and in just one exterior color: medium charcoal with orange accents. Its 1.5 liter engine with multi-port fuel injection developed 105 hp at 5400 rpm.

Chevrolet's 1985 entry into the highly competitive mini-van market—the Astro—received a luxury trim package as a 1987½ option. Also available at midyear was a new air-dam and fog light package. Standard power for the Astro continued to be the 2.5 liter four, but with a revised cylinder head with high flow ports and a redesigned intake manifold. With the optional 4.3 liter, 155 hp ''Vortex V-6'' and a new trailering package, the Astro's maximum trailering weight moved up to 6000 pounds.

With the Corvette Indy and Citation IV show cars and a new Indy racing engine, Chevrolet allowed a glimpse into the Nineties and beyond. As the oldest member of this trio, the Citation IV had been seen by millions of auto-show visitors. Its body shape, with a drag coefficient of just 0.18, gave a new meaning to the term ''aerodynamic.''

But at center stage was the Corvette Indy. ''Rarely has Chevrolet given the public such an early look at a project under development,'' said Chevrolet chief engineer Don Runkle. Plans for the Indy included all-wheel drive and steering, anti-lock braking and an ''active'' suspension system without conventional springs, shocks and stabilizer bars. Powering the Indy was a modified version of the 2.65 liter racing engine developed by Penske Racing and Chevrolet's English affiliate, Ilmor Engineering for Penske's 1986 Indy 500 assault.

1985 Monte Carlo SS Sport Coupe / Owner: Chevrolet Motor Division

1985 Celebrity Eurosport Four-Door Sedan / Owner: Chevrolet Motor Division

1985 Spectrum Two-Door Hatchback Coupe / Owner: Chevrolet Motor Division

197

1985 Nova Four-Door Sedan / Owner: Chevrolet Motor Division

1986 Camaro IROC-Z Two-Door Sport Coupe / Owner: Chevrolet Motor Division

1986 Cavalier Z24 Two-Door Hatchback / Owner: Chevrolet Motor Division

1986 Sprint Plus Four-Door Sedan / Owner: Chevrolet Motor Division

No longer shy about involvement in motor sport, Chevrolet used its forays into racing to narrow the technological gap between the future and the present. The resulting image connected with Chevrolet products not only helped sell Chevy cars and trucks, but also directly reflected upon the vehicles themselves. Technological advances and major developments from racing found their way into new product applications.

On all racing fronts, from Indy to NASCAR, Chevrolets were active participants, with no intention of easing up on the throttle. In 1986 in the IMSA GTP class, a Hendrick Motorsport Corvette took the checkered flag at Road Atlanta, ending a 17-race string of Porsche victories. On a more modest scale, one of the most memorable Chevrolet racing successes of that year took place at Lime Rock, Connecticut on May 26 when a Cavalier won the first-ever victory for a front-wheel-drive GM car in professional racing history.

Beyond the lessons learned from racing, Chevrolet also gained insight into the presentation of new automobiles from the Sprint, Spectrum and Nova. The memory of the Cavalier's poorly staged introduction combined with the lingering effects of the Citation debacle meant that future products had to be thoroughly field tested *and* available in ample supply at introduction date. In addition, hot competition within the low-priced market segment—Chevrolet's traditional market—demanded that new models be on an equivalent aesthetic and functional level with their domestic and foreign competitors.

Based in large part on the experience gained from these challenges, Chevrolet developed a new small car platform which would become known in the GM lexicon as the L-car. The first car to be born of the CPC combine, the L-car would be a uniquely Chevrolet project, with distinctive styling that would be in contrast to the homogenous appearance of GM's A- and C-body lines.

Two different L-car body configurations were developed, each with its own identity. The Corsica, available only as a four-door sedan, fell between the Cavalier and Celebrity in wheelbase, length and width. With a relatively high level

1986 Corvette Convertible / Owner: Chevrolet Motor Division

1987 Corsica Four-Door Sedan / Owner: Chevrolet Motor Division

1987 Beretta Two-Door Sport Coupe / Owner: Chevrolet Motor Division

of equipment and roomy interior dimensions, it was intended as an attractive offering for the traditional four-door sedan buyer.

Its sister car, the Beretta, shared the same basic platform, but was designed with a sportier customer in mind, one whose automotive options might include the Honda Prelude or Accord, Toyota Celica or Mazda 626 Turbo. A GT option in concert with a Z51 performance package offered stiffer suspension, 60-series Eagle GT's and a 2.8-liter V-6, making it a companion to both the Z24 and the Celebrity Eurosport.

As reliability was an important goal in the L-car project, both the Corsica and Beretta would share engine and chassis components that were derived in large part from proven Cavalier parts. The standard engine for both cars was Chevrolet's second generation ohv 2.0 liter four, uprated to 88 bhp with the addition of all-new aluminum heads with fast-burn combustion chambers and canted valves. Optional on all versions of both models was a 2.8-liter ohv V-6, which shared the four's new head design. Base transmission with the four was an Isuzu five-speed, while the six used a Getrag design.

In order to further insure a successful launch, both Corsica and Beretta were gradually eased into production after the assembly of an unprecedented 544 pilot cars. Once normal production began, some 13,000 units were scheduled for use by GM dealers and daily rental companies with approximately 3000 additional cars destined for internal use in GM and Chevrolet fleets. Official introduction of the car was set for March of 1987, allowing time for broad public evaluation and exposure.

That Chevrolet is well aware of the stiff competition awaiting the L-cars is revealed in the candor of their creators. "We realize," says project engineering manager Bob de Kruyff, "that our biggest problem was that we always tried to talk ourselves out of problems . . . . I'm tired of seeing all those black dots in *Consumer Reports*. If there is anything wrong with those cars, there really are no excuses left."

For seventy-five years Chevrolet has been shaping the way America thinks about its automobiles. That it has survived such a lengthy time span intact and indeed thriving is indicative of its own creative spirit as well as the confidence of the market which buys its products. The future Chevrolet faces today includes sobering challenges both from at home and abroad, challenges that may change the way America builds and sells its automobiles. But Chevrolet has always welcomed challenge, be it from across town or across an ocean, and whatever the future holds, Chevrolet's past will provide the resources to confront that challenge. There's no doubting that the best is still yet to come.

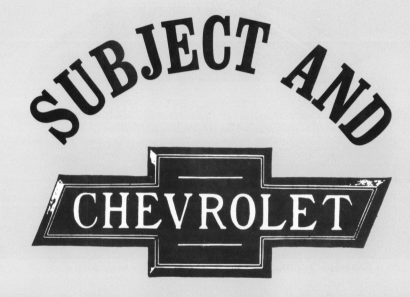

SUBJECT AND

CHEVROLET

ILLUSTRATION INDEXES

ILLUSTRATION INDEX

PHOTOGRAPHY CREDITS

Herewith Automobile Quarterly acknowledges grateful appreciation to the owners of automobiles featured in this book. Photographs are referenced by page number. All uncredited photographs are from private sources, Chevrolet files or the archives of Automobile Quarterly. Duplicate photographs are not available. Photographs may not be reproduced without permission.

Roy Query: 10, 11, 12, 13 all, 14-15, 18-19, 22-23, 35, 36-37, 42-43, 46-47, 50-51, 52 below, 53, 54, 55 above, 56-57, 58-59, 61, 62, 63, 65, 67, 68, 72-73, 76-77, 80, 81, 82-83, 87, 90, 97, 98-99, 102, 103, 106, 112, 116, 118, 122, 126-127, 129, 130-131, 132-133, 136, 137, 140, 141, 142, 144 below, 145, 147, 148, 154, 156-157 all, 160, 162-163, 165, 168, 169 above, 178-179, 182, 184 below, 185 below, 186-187, 189, 190, 191, 192, 193, 194-195 right, 197 center, 198-199, 200-201 right, 202-203.

Rick Lenz: 24, 25, 26-27, 30-31, 32-33, 34 below, 38-39, 44, 45 below, 55 below, 60, 66, 72 above and below left, 75, 78-79, 84, 85, 86, 88-89, 91, 92-93, 96, 101 all, 104-105, 107, 109, 110-111, 117, 119, 123, 124, 128, 140 above, 143, 144 above, 146, 149 all, 155 all, 158, 161, 164 below, 169 middle and below, 170-171, 175, 176m 177m 184 above, 188 below, 194 above left.

William L. Bailey: 35 above, 41, 45 above.

Richard Brown: 52 above, 120-121, 138-139.

Leslie Bird: 159, 196.